Report No. 04-INTEL-02
December 12, 2003
Audit Report

OFFICE OF THE INSPECTOR GENERAL
OF THE
DEPARTMENT OF DEFENSE

DEPUTY INSPECTOR GENERAL FOR INTELLIGENCE

DoD Security Clearance
Adjudication and Appeal Process

Acronyms

AJ	Administrative Judge
CAF	Central Adjudication Facility
DISCO	Defense Industrial Security Clearance Office
DOHA	Defense Office of Hearings and Appeals
GAO	General Accounting Office
IG DoD	Inspector General of the Department of Defense
LOD	Letter Of Denial
PERSEREC	Defense Personnel Security Research Center
PSAB	Personnel Security Appeal Board
SOR	Statement Of Reasons
U.S.C.	United States Code
USD(I)	Under Secretary of Defense for Intelligence
WHS	Washington Headquarters Services

December 12, 2003

MEMORANDUM FOR UNDER SECRETARY OF DEFENSE FOR INTELLIGENCE
GENERAL COUNSEL OF THE DEPARTMENT OF
DEFENSE

SUBJECT: Report on DoD Security Clearance Adjudication and Appeal Process
(Report No. 04-INTEL-02)

We are providing this report for review and comment. This report is the sixth in a series about DoD security clearances. We performed the audit in support of a congressional request that "the Office of the Inspector General conduct a thorough and detailed review of the security clearance investigation and adjudication processes." We considered management comments on a draft of this report when preparing the final report.

DoD Directive 7650.3 requires that all recommendations be resolved promptly. The comments of the Under Secretary of Defense for Intelligence and the General Counsel, DoD were partially responsive. We request comments on the final report by January 12, 2004.

If possible, please send management comments in electronic format (Adobe Acrobat file only) to Audam@dodig.osd.mil. Copies of the management comments must contain the actual signature of the authorizing official. We cannot accept the / Signed / symbol in place of the actual signature. If you arrange to send classified comments electronically, they must be sent over the SECRET Internet Protocol Router Network (SIPRNET).

Management comments should indicate concurrence or nonconcurrence with the finding and each applicable recommendation. Comments should describe actions taken or planned in response to agreed-upon recommendations and provide the completion dates of the actions. State specific reasons for any nonconcurrence and propose alternative actions, if appropriate.

We appreciate the courtesies extended to the staff. Questions should be directed to Mr. Robert K. West at (703) 604-9803 (DSN 664-9803) or Ms. Lois A. Therrien at (703) 602-2207 (DSN 332-2207). See Appendix F for the report distribution. The team members are listed on the inside back cover.

Thomas F. Gimble
Acting Deputy Inspector General
for Intelligence

December 12, 2003

MEMORANDUM FOR UNDER SECRETARY OF DEFENSE FOR INTELLIGENCE
GENERAL COUNSEL OF THE DEPARTMENT OF
DEFENSE

SUBJECT: Report on DoD Security Clearance Adjudication and Appeal Process
(Report No. 04-INTEL-02)

We are providing this report for review and comment. This report is the sixth in a
series about DoD security clearances. We performed the audit in support of a
congressional request that "the Office of the Inspector General conduct a thorough and
detailed review of the security clearance investigation and adjudication processes." We
considered management comments on a draft of this report when preparing the final
report.

DoD Directive 7650.3 requires that all recommendations be resolved promptly.
The comments of the Under Secretary of Defense for Intelligence and the General
Counsel, DoD were partially responsive. We request comments on the final report by
January 12, 2004.

If possible, please send management comments in electronic format (Adobe
Acrobat file only) to Audam@dodig.osd.mil. Copies of the management comments must
contain the actual signature of the authorizing official. We cannot accept the / Signed /
symbol in place of the actual signature. If you arrange to send classified comments
electronically, they must be sent over the SECRET Internet Protocol Router Network
(SIPRNET).

Management comments should indicate concurrence or nonconcurrence with the
finding and each applicable recommendation. Comments should describe actions taken
or planned in response to agreed-upon recommendations and provide the completion
dates of the actions. State specific reasons for any nonconcurrence and propose
alternative actions, if appropriate.

We appreciate the courtesies extended to the staff. Questions should be directed
to Mr. Robert K. West at (703) 604-9803 (DSN 664-9803) or Ms. Lois A. Therrien at
(703) 602-2207 (DSN 332-2207). See Appendix F for the report distribution. The team
members are listed on the inside back cover.

Thomas F. Gimble
Acting Deputy Inspector General
for Intelligence

Office of the Inspector General of the Department of Defense

Report No. 04-INTEL-02 **December 12, 2003**
(Project No. D1999AD-0079.05)

DoD Security Clearance Adjudication and Appeal Process

Executive Summary

Who Should Read This Report and Why? DoD officials who manage military, civilian, or contractor employees that require a security clearance should read this report. In particular, DoD officials responsible for security policy should read this report because it addresses a policy issue relating to disparate treatment in the adjudication and appeal process for military and civilian employees and contractor employees. In addition, the Business Initiative Council, its Steering Committee, and its Executive Directors should read this report because it relates specifically to the Business Initiative Council initiative to "Reengineer the Personnel Security Investigation" process.

Background. This report is the sixth in a series of reports on the DoD security clearance process and was initiated by a congressional request from the Chairmen of the Senate and House Committees on Armed Services in March 2000.

Executive Order No. 12958, "Classified National Security Information," April 17, 1995 (Amended March 25, 2003), prescribes a uniform system for classifying, safeguarding, and declassifying national security information that specifies that a person may have access to classified information provided a favorable determination of eligibility for access has been made, the person has signed an approved nondisclosure agreement, and the person has a need-to-know the information. Executive Order No. 12968, "Access to Classified Information," August 2, 1995, specifies Government-wide procedures for determining eligibility for access to classified information and applies to military, civilian, and contractor employees. The favorable determination of eligibility for access results in a security clearance being granted. Even after a clearance has been granted, the custodian of any classified information is responsible for controlling access by determining who has a "need-to-know."

Results. This report addresses a policy issue relating to the fairness of affording DoD civilian employees and military members with fewer due process rights in the adjudication and appeal processes than those of contractor personnel. DoD established two adjudication and appeal processes, one for military and civilian employees and one for contractor employees. The two processes result in military and civilian employees and contractor employees receiving disparate treatment in the adjudication and appeal process, with contractor employees afforded more due process rights. Establishing a single, common security clearance adjudication and appeal process and developing a single directive or regulation for that process will provide consistency in the application of the adjudicative guidelines and allow DoD to derive efficiencies and benefits. (See the Finding section of the report for the detailed recommendations.)

Management Comments and Audit Response. The Deputy Assistant Secretary of Defense (Security and Information Operations), responding for the Under Secretary of Defense for Intelligence, and the Deputy General Counsel (Legal Counsel), responding for the General Counsel, DoD, both concurred that a review of the adjudication process was appropriate, but nonconcurred that a single process for contractor, civilian, and military employees must result. The Deputy Assistant Secretary and the Deputy General Counsel also nonconcurred that a single directive for military and civilian employees and contractor employees must result. The Deputy General Counsel, however, concurred that a review of the regulations governing the security clearance process is appropriate.

Management comments were partially responsive in agreeing that the adjudication and appeal process should be reviewed as well as the regulations governing the security clearance process. Our primary concern is that the existing two adjudication and appeal processes result in disparate treatment for individuals with access to the same classified information. Also, the new security challenges facing DoD necessitate that the adjudication and appeal process be as effective and efficient as possible. We believe that the most effective and efficient way to ensure equal treatment for all employees is through a single adjudication and appeal process that is implemented by a single directive or regulation.

The draft report was issued on May 16, 2003. In response to this report, we ask that the Under Secretary of Defense for Intelligence and the General Counsel, DoD comment on whether planned or ongoing reviews of the adjudication and appeal process will result in a process that achieves equality for all parties—civilian, military, and contractor employees. We also ask them to comment specifically on why a single directive would not be the most logical as well as the most efficient and effective approach to ensure an equitable adjudication and appeal process. Comments should be received by January 12, 2004. See the Finding section of the report for a discussion of management comments and the Management Comments section of the report for the complete text of the comments.

Table of Contents

Background

This report is the sixth in a series about DoD security clearances and discusses the appeal process. The audit was initiated by a congressional request in March 2000, when the Chairmen of the Senate and House Committees on Armed Services requested further review of the security clearance investigation and adjudication processes (Appendix C). The first five reports discussed the effects of security clearances on three special access programs, security clearances for personnel in mission-critical and high-risk positions, tracking security clearance requests, the resources required to adjudicate security clearances within DoD, and the DoD adjudication process of contractor clearances. This report addresses a policy issue relating to the fairness of affording DoD civilian employees and military members with fewer due process rights in the adjudication and appeal processes than those of contractor personnel.

Right to Protect Information. The need for protecting a nation's secrets has been recognized from the earliest days of established government. In the United States, the authority to do so has historically been based on the inherent war powers of the President under the Constitution. The executive branch exercised the power to protect national defense and foreign relations information without legal formality until 1947 when an executive order was first issued under President Truman. This was followed by a series of five revisions issued under Presidents Nixon, Carter, Reagan, Clinton, and Bush. The Executive order currently in effect is Executive Order (Exec. Order) No. 12958, "Classified National Security Information," April 17, 1995 (Amended March 25, 2003). In addition to the inherent powers of the executive branch under the Constitution, the executive branch's authority to keep information secret is further recognized in five statutes: the Espionage Act, 40 Stat. 217, as amended; the National Security Act of 1947, 61 Stat. 496 (sections 401-432, title 50, United States Code [50 U.S.C. 401-432]); the Atomic Energy Act of 1954, 68 Stat. 919 (42 U.S.C. 2161-2169); the Counterintelligence and Security Enhancements Act of 1994, amending the National Security Act of 1947, 108 Stat. 3435 (50 U.S.C. 801); and the Freedom of Information Act, 5 U.S.C. 552.

Classified Information. Exec. Order No. 12958[1] prescribes a uniform system for classifying, safeguarding, and declassifying national security information. The executive order establishes three classification levels that shall be applied to information, the unauthorized disclosure of which reasonably could be expected to cause damage to national security: Top Secret, exceptionally grave damage; Secret, serious damage; and Confidential, damage.

Security Clearances and Access. Exec. Order No. 12958 states that a person may have access to classified information provided that a favorable determination of eligibility for access has been made, the person has signed an approved nondisclosure agreement, and the person has a need to know the information. The favorable determination of eligibility for access results in a security clearance being granted. Even after a clearance has been granted, the custodian of any

---

[1]These portions of the executive order were not changed in the March 25, 2003, Amended version.

classified information is responsible for controlling access by determining who has a "need-to-know."

Personnel security clearance investigations are intended to establish and maintain a reasonable threshold for trustworthiness through investigation and adjudication before granting and maintaining access to classified information. The initial investigation provides assurance that a person has not demonstrated behavior that could be a security concern. Reinvestigation is an important, formal check to help uncover changes in behavior that may have occurred after the initial clearance was granted. The standard for reinvestigation is 5 years for Top Secret, 10 years for Secret, and 15 years for Confidential clearances.

Clearance Requirements. On March 24, 1997, President Clinton approved the Temporary Eligibility Standards and Investigative Standards, and the uniform Adjudicative Guidelines as required by Exec. Order No. 12968, "Access to Classified Information," August 2, 1995. The investigative standards dictate the initial investigation and reinvestigation for access to Top Secret and Sensitive Compartmented Information and for access to Secret and Confidential information. Thirteen adjudicative guidelines were established.[2]

Adjudication Process. The adjudication process involves neither the judgment of criminal guilt nor the determination of general suitability for a given position. Instead, it assesses a person's trustworthiness and fitness for a responsibility that could, if abused, have unacceptable consequences for the national security of the United States. Eligibility for access is granted only where facts and circumstances indicate that access to classified information is clearly consistent with the national security interests of the United States. Any doubt shall be resolved in favor of the national security.

Central Adjudication Facilities and Appeal Boards. The following eight Central Adjudication Facilities (CAFs) in DoD and their corresponding appeal boards are authorized to grant, deny, or revoke eligibility for Top Secret, Secret, and Confidential security clearances and/or Sensitive Compartmented Information accesses: Army, Navy, Air Force, Washington Headquarters Services (WHS), Defense Office of Hearings and Appeals (DOHA), Joint Chiefs of Staff, Defense Intelligence Agency, and National Security Agency. In addition, the Defense Industrial Security Clearance Office (DISCO), which is part of the Defense Security Service, is authorized to grant security clearances to contractor employees.[3]

---

[2]The 13 adjudicative guidelines are allegiance to the United States; foreign influence; foreign preference; sexual behavior; personal conduct; financial considerations; alcohol consumption; drug involvement; emotional, mental, and personality disorders; criminal conduct; security violations; outside activities; and misuse of information technology systems.

[3]This issue was addressed in Inspector General of the Department of Defense Report No. D-2001-065, "DoD Adjudication of Contractor Security Clearances Granted by the Defense Security Service," February 28, 2001.

Responsibilities. The Under Secretary of Defense for Intelligence (USD[I]),[4] as the DoD senior agency official for the personnel security program, has primary responsibility for providing guidance, oversight, development, and approval for policy and procedures governing personnel security programs within DoD.[5] The General Counsel, DoD, provides advice and guidance on the legal sufficiency of procedures and standards implementing the DoD Personnel Security Program, and oversees appeal procedures to verify that the rights of individuals are being protected consistent with the Constitution, laws of the United States, executive orders, directives, or regulations that implement the DoD Personnel Security Program and that are in the interest of national security. The main responsibility of the CAFs is adjudicating personnel security background investigations. The DoD Report to Congress, "Security Clearance Denial and Revocation Procedures for Department of Defense Civilian Employees," March 1994, states that the Personnel Security Appeal Boards (PSABs) are responsible for ensuring that all DoD military and civilian employees are afforded identical safeguards in the appeal process. The DOHA Appeal Board affirms, remands, or reverses the clearance decisions handed down by the Administrative Judges (AJs) for contractor employees. Although USD(I) is responsible for providing guidance and policy for the security clearance process, the CAFs and the appeal boards are under the direction of their respective DoD Components.

Objectives

Our specific audit objective was to determine the adequacy of the adjudication and appeal process for military, civilian, and contractor employees. See Appendix A for a discussion of the audit scope and methodology. See Appendix B for prior coverage related to the audit objectives.

---

[4]Prior to May 8, 2003, the DoD Personnel Security Program function was under the cognizance of the Assistant Secretary of Defense (Command, Control, Communications, and Intelligence) (ASD[C3I]). Throughout this report, reference is made to the Under Secretary of Defense for Intelligence (USD[I]) rather than (ASD[C3I]).

[5]The Director of Central Intelligence is responsible for policy, guidance, and oversight of Sensitive Compartmented Information.

3

Two Adjudication and Appeal Processes for Obtaining DoD Security Clearances

DoD established one adjudication and appeal process for contractor employees to obtain a DoD security clearance and a second process for military and civilian employees. The two processes differ in their:

- decision authorities and levels,

- appeal board members,

- basis for the appeal process,

- personal appearance procedures,

- access to classified information when the clearance is not granted after the initial response to the Statement of Reasons (SOR), and

- degree of independence of decision authorities.

The two processes continue to exist because DoD did not develop a single process when implementing Exec. Order No. 12968, "Access to Classified Information," August 2, 1995. As a result, DoD military and civilian employees receive disparate treatment in that contractor employees are afforded more due process rights in the adjudication and appeal process.

Executive Orders Establishing Access to Classified Information

Issuing a DoD security clearance requires the protection of national security information to be balanced with the other constitutional imperatives of due process and equal protection for U.S. citizens. Three Executive orders establish standards for access to classified information and employment in the department.

Executive Order No. 10450. The first Executive order establishing standards for access to classified information was Exec. Order No. 10450, "Security Requirements for Government Employment," April 27, 1953. Exec. Order No. 10450 requires that all persons seeking the privilege of employment or those who are privileged to be employed in the Government be adjudged by mutually consistent and no less than minimum standards and procedures. It also states that the investigation of persons entering or employed in the competitive service shall primarily be the responsibility of the Office of Personnel Management, except when the head of a department or agency assumes that responsibility. The investigations of persons (including consultants, however employed) entering the employment of, or employed by, the Government other than in the competitive service shall be the responsibility of the employing department or agency.

The Supreme Court, in <u>Department of the Navy versus Egan</u>, 484 U.S. 518 (1988), states that "no one has the right to a security clearance" and that "the grant of a clearance is an affirmative act of discretion . . . only when clearly consistent with the interests of national security." It held that the "clearly consistent with the interests of national security" test indicates that "security clearance determinations should err, if they must, on the side of denials."

Executive Order No. 10865. Exec. Order No. 10865, "Safeguarding Classified Information Within Industry," February 20, 1960, provides procedures for appealing security clearance decisions for non-Government, contractor employees. It allows contractor employees to cross-examine witnesses either orally or through written interrogatories. This executive order resulted from a Supreme Court decision in <u>Greene versus McElroy</u>, 360 U.S. 474 (1959), that only with explicit authorization from either the President or Congress were the respondents empowered to deprive the petitioner of his job in a proceeding in which the petitioner was not afforded the safeguards of confrontation and cross-examination.

Executive Order No. 12968. In October 1994, the National Security Act of 1947 was amended to require the President to establish standards and procedures to govern access to classified information that would be binding on all departments, agencies, and offices of the Executive branch (50 U.S.C. 435). The law requires uniform minimum standards to ensure that employees in the Executive branch whose access to classified information was threatened with denial or termination be advised and given an adequate opportunity to respond to any adverse information before a final agency decision. Conference Committee Report language accompanying the legislation indicated that its purpose was to provide a procedure that would not base security determinations on inaccurate or unreliable information because of the effect on the careers and livelihoods of the individuals concerned and of the possibility of depriving the Government of the services of valuable employees.

Exec. Order No. 12968 followed that legislation and specifies Government-wide procedures for determining eligibility for access to classified information. Therefore, the 13 adjudicative guidelines, signed by President Clinton on March 24, 1997, apply to military, civilian, and contractor personnel. However, Exec. Order No. 12968 also states that it shall not diminish or otherwise affect the denial and revocation procedures provided to individuals covered by Exec. Order No. 10865, as amended.

Exec. Order No. 12968 also states that:

- security policies designed to protect classified information must ensure consistent, cost-effective, and efficient protection of classified information while providing fair and equitable treatment;

- eligibility for access is granted only where facts and circumstances indicate that access to classified information is clearly consistent with national security interests of the United States and that any doubts will be resolved in favor of national security; and

- background investigations and eligibility determinations conducted under the order will be mutually and reciprocally accepted by all agencies except when an agency has substantial information indicating that an employee may not satisfy the standards.

Procedures to Deny or Revoke a Security Clearance

Exec. Order Nos. 12968 and 10865 establish procedures that must be followed before a security clearance can finally be denied or revoked. Specifically, the applicant must be provided with the following information and rights:

- a written SOR detailing why access authorization may be denied or revoked,

- an opportunity to reply to the SOR in writing,

- an opportunity to appear personally and present evidence,

- the right to be represented by counsel, and

- a written notice of the final decision.

For contractor employees, Exec. Order No. 10865 also provides an opportunity to cross-examine individuals that made adverse oral or written statements about the applicant.

Two Adjudication and Appeal Processes

DoD established one adjudication and appeal process for contractor employees to obtain a DoD security clearance and a second process for military and civilian employees. Except for the opportunity to cross-examine witnesses, the executive orders prescribe similar processes for granting a clearance or issuing an SOR, responding to the SOR, making a clearance decision, and appealing the clearance decision. DoD implemented Exec. Order No. 12968 for the military and civilian employees in the revised DoD Regulation 5200.2-R (DoD 5200.2-R), "Personnel Security Program," January 1987,[6] which is issued and maintained by USD(I). DoD implemented Exec. Order No. 10865 for contractor employees through DoD Directive 5220.6 (DoDD 5220.6), "Defense Industrial Personnel Security Clearance Review Program," January 2, 1992,[7] which is administered by the General Counsel, DoD. DoDD 5220.6 creates additional requirements for the contractor process. The specific current requirements for denying or revoking a

---

[6]Revised with Changes 1, 2, and 3 as of February 23, 1996, and the Assistant Secretary of Defense (Command, Control, Communications, and Intelligence) November 10, 1998, memorandum incorporating the March 24, 1997, uniform Adjudicative Guidelines and Temporary Eligibility Standards and Investigative Standards approved by the President.

[7]Revised with Changes 1, 2, 3, and 4 as of April 20, 1999.

security clearance that were established in Exec. Order Nos. 12968 and 10865, and implemented through DoD 5200.2-R and DoDD 5220.6, are compared in Appendix D.

Decision Authorities and Levels

First Decision Made by the Adjudicator. The first decision level, in both the military and civilian process and the contractor process, is the adjudicator, a trained security specialist, who must review all the information provided by the investigation and determine whether to grant or deny the clearance (Figure 1).

The contractor process contains a two-step decision because a case analyst performs a preliminary review at DISCO, which may grant clearances for cases with little or no derogatory information, before the cases with derogatory information are transferred to the DOHA adjudicators.[8] If the adjudicator decides to deny or revoke eligibility for a security clearance, the adjudicator must prepare and provide to the individual an SOR that clearly defines the rationale for the denial or revocation, with an explanation for each relevant issue that is linked to one or more of the 13 adjudicative guidelines. If a response to the SOR is received, the information is reviewed by the adjudicator,[9] who then determines whether the response eliminates or mitigates the issues enough to grant the clearance or whether to continue the process of denial or revocation. However, the information provided to the individual for preparing the initial response to the SOR differs for the two processes (see **Basis for the Appeal Process, Basis of the Appeal**).

Appeal Decision Authorities and Levels. All applicants have the same opportunity to respond to the SOR, the first formal decision to not grant the security clearance. For the purpose of describing the events occurring in the two processes, we consider the appeal process as beginning when the adjudicator determines not to grant a clearance based on the individual's initial response to the SOR and the individual appeals that decision. The two adjudication and appeal processes define the start of the appeal process differently. The military and civilian process defines the appeal process as starting at the receipt of the applicant's response to the Letter of Denial (LOD), which is the adjudicator's determination to not grant a clearance based on the applicant's response to the SOR. The contractor process defines the appeal process as starting when either the applicant or the Department Counsel appeals the AJ decision, which was made after the applicant's second response was received, either in writing or through a personal appearance hearing.

---

[8]This issue was addressed in Inspector General of the Department of Defense Report No. D-2001-065, "DoD Adjudication of Contractor Security Clearances Granted by the Defense Security Service," February 28, 2001.

[9]DOHA Department Counsel approves the SOR before its issuance in the contractor process, and a higher-graded civilian or higher-ranking military adjudicative official approves the SOR in the military and civilian process. DOHA Department Counsel reviews the response to the SOR in the contractor process and an adjudicator performs the review in the military and civilian process. For consistency, we consider the review of the SOR by the authority that approved its issuance to be part of the adjudicator review by the first decision level authority.

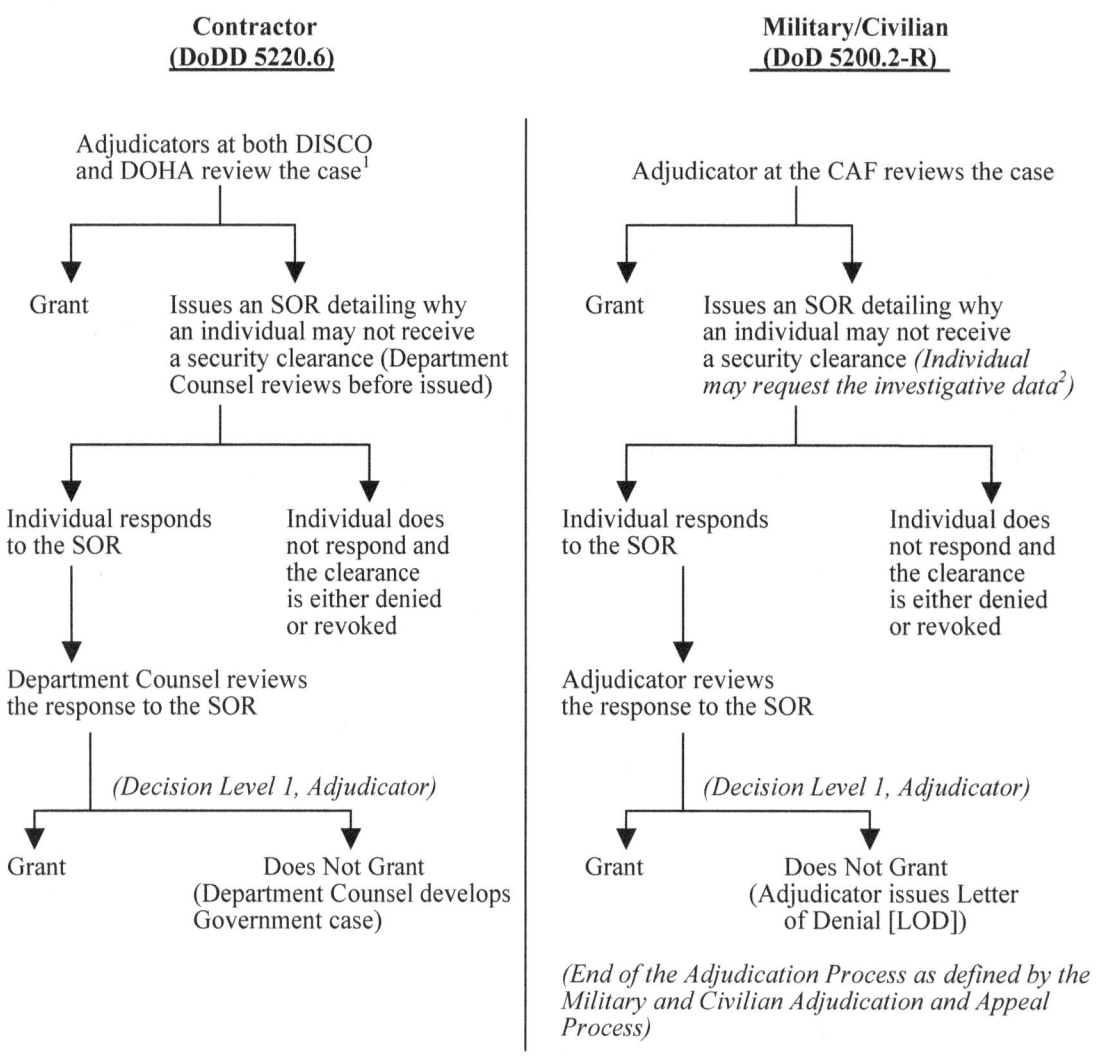

| | Contractor (DoDD 5220.6) | Military/Civilian (DoD 5200.2-R) |

[1]The contractor process provided two reviews, one by DISCO and one by DOHA, when DISCO could not grant in the first step of the first decision.

[2]The military and civilian process allows the individual to request investigative data upon issuance of the SOR. The contractor process provides this information after the decision to not grant is made based on the individual's response to the SOR (see Figure 2).

Figure 1. First Security Clearance Decision Made by the Adjudicator

The military and civilian process and the contractor process differ from the moment that the first formal determination is made to issue an SOR and the individual responds, until the final decision is made (Figure 2). The AJs and the appeal boards are part of both the contractor process and the military and civilian process; however, the role and the decision authority that the AJs and the appeal boards play in the contractor process and the military and civilian process differ. Also, the contractor process includes an additional decision level.

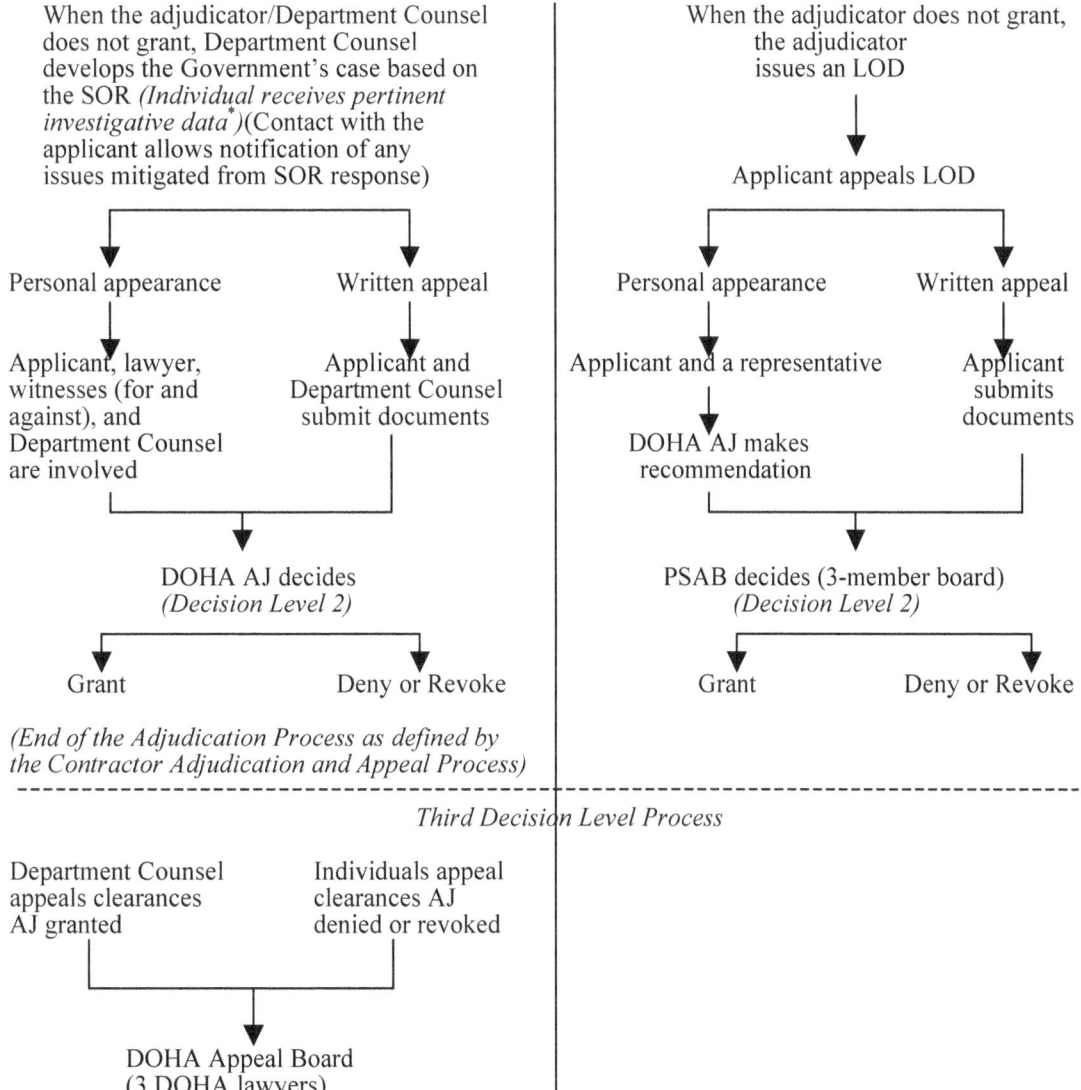

**Contractor
(DoDD 5220.6)**

**Military/Civilian
(DoD 5200.2-R)**

Second Decision Level Process

When the adjudicator/Department Counsel does not grant, Department Counsel develops the Government's case based on the SOR *(Individual receives pertinent investigative data*)*(Contact with the applicant allows notification of any issues mitigated from SOR response)

When the adjudicator does not grant, the adjudicator issues an LOD

Applicant appeals LOD

Personal appearance

Written appeal

Personal appearance

Written appeal

Applicant, lawyer, witnesses (for and against), and Department Counsel are involved

Applicant and Department Counsel submit documents

Applicant and a representative

Applicant submits documents

DOHA AJ makes recommendation

DOHA AJ decides *(Decision Level 2)*

PSAB decides (3-member board) *(Decision Level 2)*

Grant

Deny or Revoke

Grant

Deny or Revoke

(End of the Adjudication Process as defined by the Contractor Adjudication and Appeal Process)

Third Decision Level Process

Department Counsel appeals clearances AJ granted

Individuals appeal clearances AJ denied or revoked

DOHA Appeal Board (3 DOHA lawyers) make legal review *(Decision Level 3)*

Affirm

Remand (send back to AJ to reconsider)

Reverse (AJ decision deemed not in accordance with guidelines)

*The contractor process provides the pertinent investigative information when the Department Counsel cannot provide the clearance upon review of the individual's response to the SOR. This information is provided, upon the individual's request, after the issuance of the SOR in the military and civilian process.

Figure 2. Second and Third Decision Levels

Second Decision Level. When the adjudicator does not grant the clearance based on the response to the SOR, all individuals who choose to appeal the denial or revocation may do so through a written response or a personal appearance before a DOHA AJ. The AJ is a lawyer that independently hears cases to weigh the merits of the Government's security concerns versus an individual's reasons for appeal. In the contractor process, an individual AJ is the second decision level authority for both written responses and personal appearances, which may be appealed either by the contractor employee or the DOHA Department Counsel. If the AJ decision is not appealed, it becomes final. On the other hand, in the military and civilian process, if the employee makes a personal appearance, the DOHA AJ provides a recommendation to the PSAB, which is a three-member board that is the second decision level and final decision authority for all appeals.

Contractor Legal Review at Third Decision Level. The third decision level, to appeal the decision of the AJ, occurs only in the contractor employee process. If either the contractor employee or the DOHA Department Counsel appeals the AJ decision, the DOHA Appeal Board, whose primary objective is to review the case for legal error, makes the third decision. DoDD 5220.6 defines the DOHA Appeal Board's scope of review to determine whether the AJ:

- supported findings of fact with relevant evidence;

- adhered to the procedures required by Exec. Order No. 10865 and DoDD 5220.6; or

- ruled or reached conclusions that were arbitrary, capricious, or contrary to law.

Individual Decision Authorities and Decision Levels. For military and civilian employees, the second and final decision authority is a three-member board. For contractor employees, the DOHA Appeals Board is the third decision level authority. The purpose of the DOHA Appeal Board is to review the legality of the AJ decision, whereas the purpose of the Component PSAB is to make the final decision on whether to grant or deny the security clearance.

Appeal Board Members

Exec. Order No. 12968 requires that appeals be made to a high level panel composed of at least three members, two of whom shall be selected from outside the security field. The DOHA Appeal Board members are all AJs.

Defense Personnel Security Research Center (PERSEREC) Technical Report No. PERS-TR-95-002, "Appeal Board and Personal Appearance Procedures for Adverse Personnel Security Determinations in the Department of Defense," February 1995, provides policy recommendations for PSABs. The report states that the PSAB should be composed of three members. One member, a permanent president with experience in the field of personnel security, ensures that governing personnel security requirements and adjudicative criteria are considered in the board's decisions. This member also assures a measure of consistency in a board's decision making process over time. Two members, from non-security occupational specialties, reflect concerns that transcend the security field in the decision making process. The report states that the PSABs were adopted to achieve more independent due process and more consistent treatment for individuals appealing an adverse personnel security determination.

DoD 5200.2-R requires the recommended PSAB configuration. In addition, PSABs must have access to legal counsel, which may be achieved by appointing a member with a legal background. DoD 5200.2-R establishes seven[10] PSABs for the following DoD agencies: Army, Navy, Air Force, WHS, Joint Chiefs of Staff, Defense Intelligence Agency, and National Security Agency. This report did not cover the Joint Chiefs of Staff, the Defense Intelligence Agency, and the National Security Agency because the three CAFs combined adjudicated only 1 percent of the total FY 2002 cases adjudicated; therefore, the PSABs for these agencies did not hear a significant number of cases. (See Appendix E for the specific member composition of the four PSABs reviewed.) DoDD 5220.6 requires that the DOHA Appeal Board have three AJs, who are attorneys, as full-time members.

Basis for the Appeal Process

The contractor appeal process has a different basis for the appeal decision than the military and civilian process. As we previously discussed, the contractor appeal process is based on the SOR, which is generated from the adjudicator's first review of the case file. However, the military and civilian process is based on the LOD, which is generated from the adjudicator's second review of the case file when the applicant's response to the SOR, after being provided pertinent investigative data, does not justify the clearance being issued. In addition, the contractor appeal process reviews only issues that are identified in the SOR, while the military and civilian process reviews the entire case file.

Basis of the Appeal. Adjudicators at the CAFs adjudicate the information in the investigative case file and decide whether to grant access to classified information. When the adjudicator issues an SOR, both the contractor process and the military and civilian process require a written response if the adjudicator's determination is to be appealed. An adjudicator or Department Counsel (for the contractor process) reviews the written response to the SOR to determine whether the information provided eliminates or mitigates the issues and whether the clearance can be granted. The military and civilian process provides pertinent investigative data to the individual for the first response, while the contractor process provides the investigative information after the first response has been received (Figure 1, footnote 2 and Figure 2, footnote).

      Contractor Process. In the contractor process, the individual's request for a personal appearance hearing must be included in the written response to the SOR. If the written response eliminates or mitigates the issues in the SOR, the

---

[10]DoD 5200.2-R establishes an eighth PSAB under the auspices of the General Counsel, DoD, for contractors only. However, DoDD 5220.6 does not establish the DOHA Appeal Board as a DoD 5200.2-R designated PSAB.

clearance can be granted. If the written response does not eliminate or mitigate the issues in the SOR, a hearing will be held. If the response does not contain a request for a hearing, the individual has an opportunity to submit a second written response,[11] based upon all relevant and material information in the case file, and the case is assigned to an AJ for a final determination based on the written responses.

Military and Civilian Process. In the military and civilian process, if the written response does not eliminate or mitigate the issues in the SOR, the individual receives an LOD, stating the final reasons for the denial or the revocation decision, as well as methods for appealing the decision. The individual then decides whether to appeal the LOD to the Component PSAB. When an appeal is made, the employee provides additional documentary evidence in response to the remaining issues identified in the LOD to the DOHA AJ in the personal appearance hearing or to the PSAB if a hearing is not requested.

Review of Entire Case File. The uniform Adjudicative Guidelines that resulted from the implementation of Exec. Order No. 12968 state that the ultimate determination for granting or continuing eligibility for a security clearance must be an overall common-sense determination that is based upon careful consideration of the 13 adjudicative guidelines, each of which is to be evaluated in the context of the whole person, weighing all of the positive and negative factors (the whole person concept). The Adjudicative Guidelines specify that although adverse information concerning a single criterion may not be sufficient for an unfavorable determination, the individual may be disqualified if available information reflects a recent or recurring pattern of questionable judgment, irresponsibility, or emotionally unstable behavior. Notwithstanding the whole person concept, further investigation may be terminated by an appropriate adjudicative agency in the face of reliable, significant, disqualifying, adverse information.

The entire case file is not reviewed by the AJ at the second decision level for contractor employees as it is for the military and civilian employees by the PSAB. The AJ rarely sees the entire contractor employee case file; however, the AJ does see the relevant derogatory information that detracts from the contractor employee's explanation or that reflects negatively on his or her credibility. The Department Counsel presents the AJ with all of the available information supporting the issues that are a security concern as detailed in the SOR for contractor employees. The DOHA Appeal Board reviews the factual record, but it does not accept any new evidence. In contrast, in the military and civilian employee process, the PSAB members review the entire case file before a meeting, and the final decision is based on all information from the original adverse determination made by the CAF, new or explanatory information obtained from the appellant's desired course of appeal, and discussion of PSAB members' concerns.

---

[11]If the applicant did not request a hearing in his or her first response to the SOR, the Department Counsel provides the applicant with a copy of all relevant and material information and the applicant has 30 days to submit a written response. Therefore, even though the contractor process does not issue an LOD, contractor employees are allowed to respond after the initial response to the SOR, as are military and civilian employees.

Personal Appearance Procedures

The contractor appeal process and the military and civilian appeal process have different personal appearance procedures.

Contractor Personal Appearance. DoDD 5220.6 creates more specific steps and requirements for contractor employee personal appearances than required in Exec. Order No. 10865. DoDD 5220.6 establishes that when there is a personal appearance in the contractor process, contractor employees must appear before an AJ for a hearing with trial-type procedures. The contractor employee can appear before an AJ with or without counsel or a personal representative, and invite witnesses or present other evidence to rebut, extenuate, mitigate, or explain allegations made in the SOR. The DOHA Department Counsel represents the Government and presents witnesses and other evidence to establish the facts alleged in the SOR. The contractor employee has the opportunity to confront and cross-examine each witness. A verbatim transcript of the hearing is included in the contractor employee's case file. The AJ issues a written decision, which includes the facts, policies, and conclusions relating to the allegations in the SOR. The AJ decision becomes final unless either the individual or the Government appeals. Appendix D compares Exec. Order No. 10865 and DoDD 5220.6 and identifies those procedural steps that were not specifically required by the executive order.

Military and Civilian Personal Appearance. DoD 5200.2-R, change 3, February 23, 1996, implements the personal appearance hearing in the military and civilian process after the LOD is issued. DoD 5200.2-R establishes that when an individual chooses a personal appearance, the entire case file is forwarded to DOHA for review by an AJ. During the personal appearance hearing, the case is presented to the AJ by the individual or his or her representative, which may include legal counsel. The individual may make an oral presentation and respond to questions posed by his or her representative and will respond to questions posed by the AJ. The individual may submit documents relating to whether the LOD should be overturned, but will not have the opportunity to present or cross-examine witnesses. When the hearing is over, the AJ provides a written recommendation to the PSAB. That recommendation and a transcript of the case become part of the case file provided to the PSAB for a final decision. Appendix D compares Exec. Order No. 12968 and DoD 5220.2-R.

DoD Rationale for Two Personal Appearance Procedures. The DoD Report to Congress, "Security Clearance Denial and Revocation Procedures for Department of Defense Civilian Employees," March 1994, which preceded the issuance of Exec. Order No. 12968, states that personnel security investigations and adjudications are not criminal proceedings. In the report, DoD elected to treat military and civilian employees the same for purposes of security clearance adjudications and adopted a number of enhanced procedures, including personal appearance before a designated official, representation by counsel, and increased rights of access to documents upon which a proposed denial or revocation might be based. DoD concluded, however, that introducing trial-type hearing procedures similar to those enjoyed by contractor employees would be too costly and time-consuming.

Access to Classified Information When the Clearance is Not Granted After the Initial Response to the SOR

The contractor process allows contractor employees with a security clearance to access classified information when the clearance is not granted after the initial response to the SOR. The clearance is revoked only when either the AJ or the DOHA Appeal Board makes the final determination. Only USD(I) may suspend a contractor employee's clearance during the appeal process with concurrence of the General Counsel, DoD. However, military and civilian security clearances that are questionable must be suspended when the LOD is issued if the commander or head of the organization has not previously suspended them.

Contractor Process. Exec. Order No. 10865 does not directly address suspension of access while awaiting the final decision. Section 3 states that, except as provided in section 9, an authorization for access to classified information cannot be finally denied or revoked absent the procedural safeguards specified in the order. Exec. Order No. 10865, section 9, states:

> Nothing contained in this order shall be deemed to limit or affect the responsibility and powers of the head of the Department to deny or revoke access to a specific classification category if the security of the nation so requires. Such authority may not be delegated and may be exercised only when the head of a Department determines that the procedures prescribed in sections 3, 4, and 5[12] cannot be invoked consistently with national security and such determination shall be conclusive.

DoDD 5220.6 establishes a process to suspend access of contractor employees that have a security clearance prior to the final security clearance decision and places the suspension authority as the USD(I), with concurrence of the General Counsel, DoD. However, the directive does not require that access to classified information by contractors be suspended until the appeal has been completed if the Department Counsel cannot grant the clearance based on the individual's response to the SOR. DoDD 5220.6, subsection 6.4, states:

> Whenever there is a reasonable basis for concluding that an applicant's continued access to classified information poses an imminent threat to national interest, any security clearance held by the applicant may be suspended by the ASD(C^3I) [Assistant Secretary of Defense (Command, Control, Communications, and Intelligence)], with concurrence of the GC [General Counsel], DoD, pending a final clearance decision. This suspension may be rescinded by the same authorities upon presentation of additional information that conclusively demonstrates that an imminent threat to the national interest no longer exists. Procedures in enclosure 3 shall be expedited whenever an applicant's security clearance has been suspended pursuant to this subsection.

---

[12]Section 3 covers the appeal process, section 4 deals with the opportunity to cross-examine persons that have made oral or written statements adverse to the individual, and section 5 pertains to records and physical evidence.

Military and Civilian Process. Change 3 to DoD 5200.2-R, February 23, 1996, establishes that the commander or head of the organization may suspend a security clearance for access to classified information and assign the individual to nonsensitive duties when the SOR is issued; however, the regulation requires the security clearance to be revoked when the LOD is issued if it had not been suspended when the SOR was issued.

Degree of Independence of Decision Authorities

The contractor process does not use the separation of the adjudication and the appeal decision authorities that is required by the military and civilian process.

Contractor Organizational Structure. The Director, DOHA, supervises all DOHA operations and is responsible for administering the Defense Industrial Personnel Security Clearance Review Program. DoDD 5220.6 states that the AJs and the appeal board members will have the requisite independence to render fair and impartial decisions consistent with DoD policy. The PERSEREC Technical Report 93-6, "Due Process for Adverse Personnel Security Determinations in the DoD," September 1993, states that for appeals by Defense contractor employees, the adjudicators, the AJs, and the members of the appeal board function independently. Further, the report states that the appeal board controls against bias, especially from superior authority, because it has three members, and that the legal staff at DOHA is highly trained and cognizant of its responsibility to decide cases without bias. The report states that the Director, DOHA, has administrative responsibility for these functions, but is not directly involved in substantive matters related to specific cases. The director performs the second-level review for all adjudicators, AJs, and department counsel representatives; the director is also the first-level reviewer for the Chief AJ; the Chief, Department Counsel; and all three appeal board members (Figure 3).

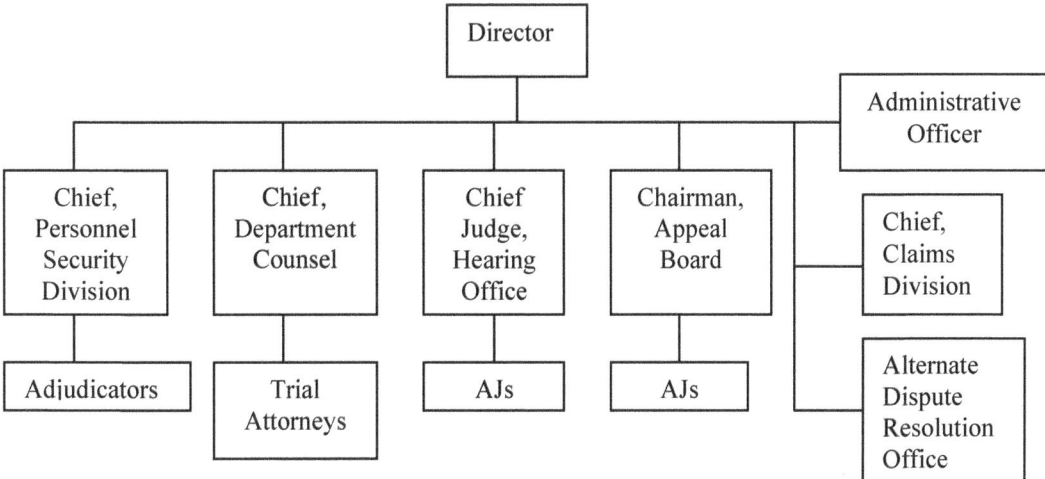

Figure 3. DOHA Organizational Chart

Military and Civilian Organizational Structure. The adjudicative decision authorities for the military and civilian process are the adjudicators and the PSAB members. Adjudicators are employee positions located in the CAFs of the pertinent Components. PSAB members are "as needed" positions, so their service on the board is in addition to their regular duties.

DoD 5200.2-R requires each Component that has a CAF to also have a PSAB that is separate from its respective CAF. The relationship between the CAF and its PSAB is administrative in that once an appeal is made, any case documents needed by the PSAB are forwarded by the CAF. DoD 5200.2-R specifically states that officials from the CAF will neither serve as members of the board nor communicate with board members concerning the merits of an open case. The PSAB either sustains or overturns the original determination of the CAF; therefore, it must be separate.

One of the four PSABs that we reviewed was not completely separate from the CAFs, but was not connected organizationally by more than one of the three members. The Army, Navy and Air Force CAFs and PSABs are in separate organizations, but the PSAB presidents' position in the WHS is within the same organization as the CAF, as shown in the table.

	Organizational Relationship of CAF and PSAB Presidents	
	CAF Adjudicators	PSAB President
Army	Intelligence and Security Command	Assistant Secretary of the Army (Manpower and Reserve Affairs)
Navy	Naval Criminal Investigative Service[1]	Office of the Chief of Naval Operations
		Special Assistant for Naval Investigative Matters and Security[1]
		Assistant for Information and Personnel Security[2]
Air Force	Secretary of the Air Force Administrative Assistant	Judge Advocate General
		General Law Division
WHS	Directorate for Personnel Security	Directorate for Personnel Security
		Security Directorate

[1] The same individual fills both positions.
[2] This individual is also the Deputy Assistant Director, Information and Personnel Security Programs, Naval Criminal Investigative Service.

DoD Rationale for Two Adjudication and Appeal Processes

The two processes continue to exist because DoD did not develop a single process for military, civilian, and contractor employees when implementing Exec. Order No. 12968. The DoD Report to Congress, "Security Clearance Denial and Revocation Procedures for Department of Defense Civilian Employees," March 1994, resulted from a partial review of the military and civilian process in response to section 1183 of the National Defense Authorization Act for FY 1994, which required the Secretary of Defense to conduct a review of the procedural safeguards available to DoD civilian employees that are facing denial or revocation of security clearances. However, DoD reviewed only whether military and civilians could be given the same process as contractor employees.

DoD military and civilian employees receive disparate treatment in that contractor employees are afforded more due process rights in the adjudication and appeal process. The DoD Report to Congress, March 1994, also states that DoD assumes that, for a contractor employee, the denial or revocation of a clearance was more likely to result in loss of current employment, while a DoD civilian employees was more likely to be employed in another position not requiring a security clearance. For this reason, the report states that contractor employees have a greater interest in additional procedural safeguards than DoD civilians. However, within DoD this may no longer be the case because downsizing, in the 1990s, greatly reduced the ability of military and civilian employees to be employed in positions that do not require a security clearance. Consequently, the denial or revocation of a security clearance is also likely to result in a loss of current employment for military and civilian employees as well as for contractor employees.

Conclusion

Whether an individual is a contractor, a civilian, or a military employee, the DoD security clearance allows access to the same categories of information. Therefore, access requirements and the application of the adjudicative guidelines for DoD security clearances should be consistent regardless of the process through which the clearance is received. Additionally, DoD may not be achieving the efficiencies and benefits that would be derived from a single consistent adjudication and appeal process for obtaining a security clearance. Policymakers need to consider the fundamental fairness of affording civilian and military employees with fewer due process rights than contractor employees.

Currently the military and civilian adjudication process ends upon the individual's first written response to the SOR and the first decision level authority's final determination to grant a clearance or issue an LOD. However, the contractor process does not end the adjudication process until the second decision level authority's final determination after the individual's second written response to the SOR or the personal appearance hearing. In addition, more than 40 years have passed since the contractor process was developed for Exec. Order No. 10865, and DoD is facing new security challenges, in the homeland and abroad, as evidenced by the September 11, 2001, terrorist attacks and threats from countries that have weapons of mass destruction. Therefore, we believe that DoD needs to establish a single, consistent adjudication and appeal process for obtaining a DoD security clearance for military, civilian, and contractor employees by reengineering the entire process and developing a single directive or regulation for the process.

Recommendations are in line with an ongoing Business Initiative Council initiative to improve the efficiency of the Personnel Security Investigation process. The Business Initiative Council was established by the Secretary of Defense on June 18, 2001, with the mission to improve the efficiency of the DoD business operations by identifying and implementing business reform actions, which allow savings to be reallocated to higher efforts. The Under Secretary of Defense for Acquisition, Technology, and Logistics is the Chairman of the Business Initiative Council.

The Business Initiative Council approved the sixth set of initiatives on September 4, 2002. One of the initiatives is "Reengineering Personnel Security Investigation," which seeks relief to the burdensome and slow processes associated with conducting personnel security investigations. The Business Initiative Council is engaged in a two-phased approach relating to that initiative, which initially includes gathering quick-fix remedies to obstacles. After implementing the quick-fix remedies, the second phase will review and redesign the end-to-end process, from request to adjudication. The reengineering effort is expected to improve timeliness and reduce long-term costs. We believe this report, as well as other Inspector General of the Department of Defense (IG DoD) reports on the DoD personnel security process identified in Appendix B, will greatly assist the Business Initiative Council in its endeavor to reengineer the personnel security investigative process.

Management Comments on the Finding and Audit Response

Under Secretary of Defense for Intelligence Comments. The Deputy Assistant Secretary of Defense (Security and Information Operations), responding for the Under Secretary of Defense for Intelligence, states that the report lacks clarity and leads to a misunderstanding of the adjudicative process. The Deputy Assistant Secretary states that DoD has a major effort underway to improve its personnel security program and that a review of the adjudication process, targeted for completion in the fall, was part of that review. The Deputy Assistant Secretary also states that DoD had proposed changes to the adjudication guidelines to the interagency group reviewing personnel security policy issues, and that Congress has proposed tasking the Secretary of Defense and the Director, Central Intelligence Agency to submit a joint report on the usefulness and effectiveness of the security background investigations and security clearance procedures.

Audit Response. The Deputy Assistant Secretary of Defense did not specify what was unclear in the report and what would lead to a misunderstanding of the adjudicative process. The initiatives that the Deputy Assistant Secretary of Defense alluded to concerning the personnel security program are encouraging; however, she did not state whether those initiatives will ensure that all parties—

civilian, military, and contractor employees—will receive equal treatment in the adjudication and appeal process. The main theme of our report is that two separate processes currently result in disparate treatment for contractor employees and civilian and military employees, even though a DoD security clearance allows them access to the same categories of information, given that they each have a valid need-to-know.

General Counsel Comments. The DoD Deputy General Counsel (Legal Counsel), responding for the General Counsel, DoD, states that "the analysis contained in the report is fundamentally flawed and infused with major factual errors and misconceptions." The Deputy General Counsel (Legal Counsel) states further that the report makes a fundamental error in describing the adjudication and appeal process—specifically in comparing the procedures available to contractor employees versus military and civilian employees. He states that the report erroneously equates a contractor employee's case being referred for further processing with issuing an LOD to military and civilian employees, leading to a conclusion that an extra step exists in one of the processes, which the Deputy General Counsel (Legal Counsel) concludes "is incorrect as a matter of fact and as a matter of law, and this error alone essentially destroys the value of the analysis contained in the report." The Deputy General Counsel (Legal Counsel) also states that the report "presents a misleading description of the organization and legal structure of the adjudication facilities within the Department." He states that Component adjudication facilities and DOHA operate under rules and in an environment that protects their impartiality and independence from improper efforts to influence decisions in individual cases. He states that both organizational approaches are legally sound.

Audit Response. The comments provided by the DoD Deputy General Counsel (Legal Counsel), include a statement that equating referral of ". . . a contractor employee's case for further processing and issuing a Letter of Denial to government employees and military personnel" is "incorrect as a matter of fact and as a matter of law. . . ." The Deputy General Counsel (Inspector General) reviewed the recommendations contained in this audit report and found no legal problems with those recommendations. At the direction of the Inspector General, the Deputy General Counsel (Inspector General) gave the Deputy General Counsel (Legal Counsel) an opportunity to support or clarify this statement. The Deputy General Counsel (Legal Counsel) declined the opportunity.

In response to the comments of the Deputy General Counsel (Legal Counsel), the Deputy General Counsel (Inspector General) opined:

> The Deputy General Counsel (Legal Counsel) takes no issue with the fact that two separate processes result in disparate treatment for contractor employees versus civilian and military personnel of the Department of Defense (i.e., fewer due process rights for DoD personnel). Just as the Supreme Court found that additional due process must be afforded to contractor employees who could be deprived of their employment when denied a security clearance, DoD personnel likewise have their employment at risk in such circumstances. Therefore, policymakers should consider providing the same due process to DoD personnel.

In our analysis of the adjudication and appeal processes, we consider a decision to have occurred whenever the decision level authority had the ability to grant a clearance, even if the decision level authority did not have the ability to deny a clearance. In that context, when comparing the number of times a decision to grant a clearance can be made, the contractor process allows an additional opportunity for a decision.

In response to the Deputy General Counsel (Legal Counsel)'s comments on the report's description of the contractor versus military and civilian organizational and legal structure, the report identifies the two different structures and states that DoD 5200.2-R requires the separation of the CAFs and the PSABs in the military and civilian process. Further, the report does not imply that one organizational structure is more sufficient or legally sound than the other.

Recommendations, Management Comments, and Audit Response

We recommend that the Under Secretary of Defense for Intelligence, in coordination with the General Counsel, DoD:

1. Reengineer the adjudication and appeal process by establishing a single, common security clearance process for military, civilian, and contractor employees.

Under Secretary of Defense for Intelligence Comments. The Deputy Assistant Secretary of Defense (Security and Information Operations), responding for the Under Secretary of Defense for Intelligence, nonconcurred stating that the recommendation was generic and applicable to almost every Government program and that the report does not offer a persuasive basis to establish a single process. However, as discussed under Management Comments on the Finding, the Deputy Assistant Secretary of Defense, in discussing several initiatives underway to improve the adjudication process and the personnel security program as a whole, concurred that a review of the process is appropriate.

General Counsel Comments. The DoD Deputy General Counsel (Legal Counsel), responding for the General Counsel, DoD, concurred that a review of the adjudication and appeal process is appropriate, but did not concur with the recommendation that a single process applicable to civilian and military as well as contractor employees must result. The Deputy General Counsel states that the report notes that the contractor process differs from the process for civilian and military employees, but provides no rationale for the need to unify them. The Deputy General Counsel states that contractor employees have a different legal status from civilian and military employees, and that the procedures available to contractor employees in a wide range of dealings with the Government differ significantly from those individuals who have a direct employment relationship with the Government.

Audit Response. The Deputy Assistant Secretary of Defense (Security and Information Operations) and the Deputy General Counsel comments were partially responsive in agreeing that the adjudication and appeal process needs review. Furthermore, the initiatives described by the Deputy Assistant Secretary that are underway seem particularly encouraging. Our primary concern is that the existing processes result in disparate treatment for individuals that are granted access to the same classified information. Any review and reengineering of the adjudication and appeal process should result in a process that provides equal treatment for all parties—military and civilian employees and contractor employees. In addition, the new security challenges facing DoD necessitate an effective and efficient adjudication and appeal process. We believe that the most efficient and effective way to ensure equal treatment for all employees is through a single adjudication and appeal process. In response to this report, we request that the Under Secretary for Intelligence and the General Counsel, DoD, provide comments that explain whether the ongoing reviews or those planned will result in an adjudication and appeals process that achieves equality for all parties—civilian, military, and contractor employees.

2. Develop a single directive or regulation for the DoD security clearance process.

Under Secretary of Defense for Intelligence Comments. The Deputy Assistant Secretary of Defense (Security and Information Operation), responding for the Under Secretary of Defense for Intelligence, nonconcurred that a single directive or regulation is appropriate. The Deputy Assistant Secretary states that the recommendation was generic and applicable to almost every Government program and that the report does not offer a persuasive basis to establish a single directive.

General Counsel Comments. The DoD Deputy General Counsel (Legal Counsel), responding for the General Counsel, DoD, concurred that a review of the regulations governing the security clearance process is appropriate but nonconcurred that a single directive or regulation applicable to military and civilian employees and contractor employees must result. The Deputy General Counsel states that the current regulatory structure appears to work well and does not cause confusion among those who use the regulations.

Audit Response. The Deputy Assistant Secretary of Defense (Security and Information Operation) comments were partially responsive. Although not specifically stated, the Deputy Assistant Secretary comments relating to ongoing reviews of the adjudication and personnel security process imply that the regulations governing the security clearance process would also be reviewed. The DoD Deputy General Counsel (Legal Counsel) comments were partially responsive in agreeing that a review of the regulations governing the security clearance process was in order. As stated in our audit response to Recommendation 1., our main objective is to achieve a process that treats all parties that are entrusted with the same information equally. We believe a single process, implemented by a single directive or regulation, is the best way to achieve that end. In response to this report, we request that the Under Secretary of Defense for Intelligence and the General Counsel, DoD, comment specifically on the merits of a single directive or regulation for the DoD security process and explain why that approach would not be the most logical as well as the most efficient and effective way to ensure an equitable appeals and adjudication process for all parties.

Appendix A. Scope and Methodology

We reviewed the executive orders, implementing guidance, studies, pertinent reports, and the operations of the eight CAFs for the adjudication and appeal processes for military, civilian, and contractor employees. We also reviewed the operation and makeup of four of the seven PSABs and the DOHA Appeals Board. In addition, we obtained the adjudication statistics for the CAFs from the FYs 2001 and 2002 Spend Plan reports.

We performed this audit from May 2000 through April 2003 in accordance with generally accepted government auditing standards.

We did not review the management control program related to the overall audit objective because DoD recognized the personnel security investigations program as a material weakness in its FY 2000 Statement of Assurance and its FY 2002 Performance and Accountability Report.

To determine the differences in the military and civilian and the contractor adjudication and appeal processes for being granted or denied a DoD security clearance, we compared the specific steps and decision levels in the appeal processes with the executive orders to determine the differences generated by the executive orders and those generated by DoDD 5220.6 and DoD 5200.2-R that implement the executive orders. We also reviewed studies by the PERSEREC that reviewed personnel security clearance adjudicative information and other pertinent reports.

The audit project leader participated in the Personnel Security Overarching Integrated Process Team, established by the Deputy Secretary of Defense on November 30, 1999, to "Pioneer a different path to solve the crisis of the continuing personnel security investigations backlog, and sell it," and the Personnel Security Investigation Process Review Team, established by the Deputy Secretary of Defense on June 1, 2000, to clearly baseline the current status of reforming the personnel security investigation process, to determine when the process is expected to get well, and to provide any recommendations to expedite the reform effort. The scope of the audit was not limited in this regard because neither team reviewed the specific steps of the adjudication and appeal process.

We did not use computer-processed data to perform this audit.

General Accounting Office High-Risk Area. The General Accounting Office has identified several high-risk areas in the Department of Defense. This report provides coverage of the Strategic Human Capital Management high-risk area.

Appendix B. Prior Coverage

During the last 10 years, the General Accounting Office (GAO) issued 3 reports; the IG DoD issued 12 reports; the PERSEREC issued 7 reports; and the Joint Security Commission II, the Commission on Protecting and Reducing Government Secrecy, and the Joint Security Commission issued 1 report each on the DoD Personnel Security Program. Unrestricted GAO reports can be accessed over the Internet at http://www.gao.gov. Unrestricted IG DoD reports can be accessed at http://www.dodig.osd.mil/audit/reports.

GAO

GAO Report No. GAO-01-465, "DoD Personnel: More Consistency Needed in Determining Eligibility for Top Secret Security Clearances," April 18, 2001

GAO Report No. NSIAD-00-215, "DoD Personnel: More Actions Needed to Address Backlog of Security Clearance Reinvestigations," August 24, 2000

GAO Report No. NSIAD-00-12, "DoD Personnel: Inadequate Personnel Security Investigations Pose National Security Risks," October 27, 1999

IG DoD

IG DoD Report No. D-2003-112, "Homeland Security: Contracting Practices of the Defense Security Service for Personnel Security Investigations," June 27, 2003 (FOR OFFICIAL USE ONLY)

IG DoD Report No. D-2001-136, "Defense Clearance and Investigations Index Database," June 7, 2001

IG DoD Report No. D-2001-112, "Acquisition Management of the Joint Personnel Adjudication System," May 5, 2001

IG DoD Report No. D-2001-065, "DoD Adjudication of Contractor Security Clearances Granted by the Defense Security Service," February 28, 2001

IG DoD Report No. D-2001-019, "Program Management of the Defense Security Service Case Control Management System," December 15, 2000

IG DoD Report No. D-2001-008, "Resources of DoD Adjudication Facilities," October 30, 2000

IG DoD Report No. D-2000-134, "Tracking Security Clearance Requests," May 30, 2000

IG DoD Report No. D-2000-111, "Security Clearance Investigative Priorities," April 5, 2000

IG DoD Report No. D-2000-072, "Expediting Security Clearance Background Investigations for Three Special Access Programs" (U), January 31, 2000 (SECRET)

IG DoD Report No. 98-124, "Department of Defense Adjudication Program," April 27, 1998

IG DoD Report No. 98-067, "Access Reciprocity Within DoD Special Access Programs" (U), February 10, 1998 (CONFIDENTIAL)

IG DoD Report No. 97-196, "Personnel Security in the Department of Defense," July 25, 1997

PERSEREC

PERSEREC, Technical Report 02-4, "Quality Assurance in Defense Adjudication: An Adjudicator Workshop for Defining and Assessing Quality," March 2003

PERSEREC, Technical Report 00-4, "Security Clearances and the Protection of National Security Information Law and Procedures," November 2000

PERSEREC, Technical Report 00-2, "Adjudicative Guidelines and Investigative Standards in the Department of Defense," September 2000

PERSEREC, Technical Report 00-1, "An Analysis of Clearance Review Decisions by the Defense Office of Hearings and Appeals," September 2000

PERSEREC, PERS-TR-95-002, "Appeal Board and Personal Appearance Procedures for Adverse Personnel Security Determinations in the Department of Defense," February 1995

PERSEREC, PERS-TR-94-002, "Standardizing Procedures for Notifying Individuals of an Adverse Personnel Security Determination in the Department of Defense," September 1994

PERSEREC, Technical Report-93-6, "Due Process for Adverse Personnel Security Determinations in the DoD," September 1993

Other Reports

Joint Security Commission II, "Report of the Joint Security Commission II," August 24, 1999

Commission on Protecting and Reducing Government Secrecy, Senate Document 105-2, "Report of the Commission on Protecting and Reducing Government Secrecy," March 3, 1997

Joint Security Commission, "Redefining Security," February 28, 1994

Appendix C. Congressional Request

Congress of the United States
Washington, DC 20515

March 14, 2000

Mr. Donald Mancuso
Deputy Inspector General
Department of Defense
400 Army-Navy Drive
Arlington, VA. 22202-2884

Dear Mr. Mancuso:

We are writing to request that you conduct an investigation of recent reports regarding alleged problems with the DOD's system for granting security clearances.

In an October 1999 report, the General Accounting Office (GAO) concluded that DOD investigative failures created "risks to national security by granting security clearances based on incomplete investigations." GAO found that such problems stemmed from ill-advised efforts by the Defense Security Service (DSS) to streamline the investigation process and problems with the new automation system at DSS. As a result, GAO found that in June 1999, about 600,000 DOD clearances were based on outdated investigations.

We are also deeply troubled by reports that the DOD security clearance adjudication process may be flawed. Recent articles in *USA Today* have alleged that defense contractor employees with criminal backgrounds, including convicted felons, have been granted security clearances. Although the Department initially denied clearances for some of these individuals, the clearances were subsequently approved by the Defense Office of Hearings and Appeals (DOHA).

In 1997, the President approved uniform adjudication guidelines for determining eligibility for access to classified information. While these guidelines were a step toward consistency in the adjudication process, their application may be inconsistent. The DOD/IG recognized this in an April 1998 report, which recommended the implementation of a peer review system to ensure compliance and consistent application of policies and procedures across the adjudication facilities. It appears that such a system has not been implemented.

Based on these, and other facts, we believe that the system for granting DOD security clearances needs further examination. Therefore, we request that the Office of the Inspector General conduct a thorough and detailed review of the security clearance investigation and adjudication processes, to include an investigation of the backlog at DSS, the reasons for this backlog and plans to deal with it; problems DSS has experienced in developing and operationalizing the Case Control Management System; and the consistency of application of adjudication guidelines by each of the adjudication facilities. In conducting this review, we ask you to evaluate and comment on the work completed, and ongoing, by the GAO, as well as the reports that have appeared in the press. In addition, we request that you revisit your earlier recommendations regarding peer review, to determine whether such a system can and should be implemented. We understand that some corrective actions may have been initiated already by DSS and the adjudication facilities. Therefore, we ask that you also assess the progress made to date in these corrective efforts.

We appreciate your undertaking this review to determine whether DOD is adequately addressing identified weaknesses in the security clearance process. If you have any questions regarding this request please contact Mr. Peter Berry of the House Armed Services Committee staff at (202) 225-3040, or Mr. Eric Thoemmes of the Senate Armed Services Committee staff at (202) 224-9349.

Thank you for your assistance in this matter.

Sincerely,

John W. Warner
Chairman
Senate Committee on Armed Services

Floyd D. Spence
Chairman
House Committee on Armed Services

Appendix D. Comparison of Executive Order Nos. 12968 and 10865, DoD 5200.2-R and DoDD 5220.6

Authorization for access may not be finally denied or revoked unless the individual has been given the following. The section references for each document are provided in Appendixes D1 through D4.

	Military and Civilian		Contractor	
	Exec. Order 12968 (D1)	DoD 5200.2-R (D2)	Exec. Order 10865 (D3)	DoDD 5220.6 (D4)
Provided a written SOR as to why access may be denied or revoked.	5.2(a)(1)	8-201.a.	3(1)	4.3.1. E3.1.3.
Provided any documents, records, and reports upon which a denial or revocation is based. *(CAFs provide evidence upon the individual's request for answering the SOR, see DoD 5200.2-R. Department Counsel provides evidence to all individuals after response to the SOR, see DoDD 5220.6.)*	5.2(a)(2)	8-201.a.		E3.1.7. E3.1.13.
Provided the opportunity to reply in writing to the SOR.	5.2(a)(4)	8-201.b.	3(2)	4.3.2. E3.1.4.
Review the applicant's answer to the SOR.	5.2(a)(5)	8-201.c.		E3.1.6.
Provided written response stating the final reason(s) for the unfavorable results of the review (LOD).	5.2(a)(5)	8-201.c.		
Provided the identity of the deciding authority.	5.2(a)(5)			
Provided the opportunity to appeal (the LOD to the PSAB).	5.2(a)(4) 5.2(a)(5)	8-201.d.		
No Hearing Provided an opportunity to appeal (respond) in writing	5.2(a)(6)	8-201.d. 8-201.d.(1)		E3.1.7.

	Military and Civilian		Contractor	
	Exec. Order 12968 (D1)	DoD 5200.2-R (D2)	Exec. Order 10865 (D3)	DoDD 5220.6 (D4)
Appeal to a high level panel, which shall be composed of at least three members, two of whom shall be selected from outside the security field.	5.2(a)(6)	8-201.d. 8-201.d.(1)		
If the applicant or Department Counsel has not requested a hearing, the case shall be assigned to an AJ for a clearance decision based on the written record.				E3.1.7.

Hearing

Provided an opportunity to be represented by counsel or other representative at own expense.	5.2(a)(3)	8-201.a.(1) N-5.a.	3(5)	4.3.4.
Provided an opportunity to appear personally and to present relevant documents, materials, and information (evidence).	5.2(a)(7)	8-201.d.(2) N-5.b. N-5.c.	3(3)	4.3.4. E3.1.3. E3.1.8. E3.1.15.
Department Counsel is responsible for presenting witnesses and other evidence to establish facts alleged in the SOR that have been controverted.				E3.1.14.
The applicant is responsible for presenting witnesses and other evidence to rebut, explain, extenuate, or mitigate facts admitted by the applicant or proven by Department Counsel.				E3.1.15.
An opportunity to cross-examine persons either orally or through written interrogatories (who have made oral or written statements adverse to the applicant relating to a controverted issue) on matters not relating to the characterization in the SOR of any organization or individual other than the applicant.			3(6) 4(a)	4.3.3. E3.1.16.

	Military and Civilian		Contractor	
	Exec. Order 12968 (D1)	DoD 5200.2-R (D2)	Exec. Order 10865 (D3)	DoDD 5220.6 (D4)
The appellant will not have the opportunity to present or cross-examine witnesses.		N-5.d.		
The SOR may be amended at the hearing by the AJ.				E3.1.17.
The Federal Rules of Evidence shall serve as a guide. Relevant and material evidence may be received subject to rebuttal, and technical rules of evidence may be relaxed to permit the development of a full and complete record.				E3.1.19.
A verbatim transcript shall be made part of the applicant's or employee's security record (unless such an appearance occurs in the presence of the appeals panel).	5.2(a)(7)			E3.1.24.
AJ provides a recommendation to the PSAB.		8-201.d.(2) N-6		
Provided a written notice of the final decision. *(PSAB decision for Exec. Order No. 12968 and DoD 5200.2-R, but the AJ decision for DoDD 5220.6.)*	5.2(a)(6)	8-201.e. N-6.	3(7)	4.3.5. E3.1.25.
The applicant or the Department Counsel may appeal the AJ decision.				E3.1.28.
The Appeal Board shall be provided the case record. No new evidence shall be received or considered.				E3.1.29.
The appeal brief, submitted to the Appeal Board, must state the specific issue or issues being raised, and cite specific portions of the case record supporting any alleged error.				E3.1.30.

| | Military and Civilian | | Contractor | |
	Exec. Order 12968 (D1)	DoD 5200.2-R (D2)	Exec. Order 10865 (D3)	DoDD 5220.6 (D4)
A written reply brief may be submitted.				E3.1.30.
The Appeal Board shall address the material issues raised by the parties to determine whether harmful error occurred.				E3.1.32.
The Appeal Board shall issue a written clearance decision addressing the material issues raised on appeal. A copy shall be provided to the parties.				E3.1.33. E3.1.34.
A clearance decision is considered final when the Appeal Board affirms or reverses the AJ clearance decision so a clearance is granted or denied.				E3.1.36.
Upon remand, the case file shall be assigned to an AJ for correction of error(s) in accordance with the Appeal Board's clearance decision. The assigned AJ shall make a new clearance decision that shall be provided to the parties. The clearance decision after remand may be appealed.				E3.1.35.

Appendix D1. Executive Order No. 12968, Section 5.2(a)

<u>Sec. 5.2. Review Proceedings for Denials or Revocations of Eligibility for Access.</u> (a) Applicants and employees who are determined to not meet the standards for access to classified information established in section 3.1 of this order shall be:

(1) provided as comprehensive and detailed a written explanation of the basis for that conclusion as the national security interests of the United States and other applicable law permit;

(2) provided within 30 days, upon request and to the extent the documents would be provided if requested under the Freedom of Information Act (5 U.S.C. 552) or the Privacy Act (3 U.S.C. 552a), as applicable, any documents, records, and reports upon which a denial or revocation is based;

(3) informed of their right to be represented by counsel or other representative at their own expense; to request any documents, records, and reports as described in section 5.2 (a) (2) upon which a denial or revocation is based; and to request the entire investigative file, as permitted by the national security and other applicable law, which, if requested, shall be promptly provided prior to the time set for a written reply;

(4) provided a reasonable opportunity to reply in writing to, and to request a review of, the determination;

(5) provided written notice of and reasons for the results of the review, the identity of the deciding authority, and written notice of the right to appeal;

(6) provided an opportunity to appeal in writing to a high level panel, appointed by the agency head, which shall be comprised of at least three members, two of whom shall be selected from outside the security field. Decisions of the panel shall be in writing, and final except as provided in subsection (b) of this section; and

(7) provided an opportunity to appear personally and to present relevant documents, materials, and information at some point in the process before an adjudicative or other authority, other than the investigating entity, as determined by the agency head. A written summary or recording of such appearance shall be made part of the applicant's or employee's security record, unless such appearance occurs in the presence of the appeals panel described in subsection (a)(6) of this section.

Appendix D2. DoD 5200.2-R, Section 8-201 and Appendix N

8-201 Unfavorable Administrative Action Procedures

Except as provided for below, no unfavorable administrative action shall be taken under the authority of this Regulation unless the individual concerned has been:

a. Provided a written statement of the reasons (SOR) as to why the unfavorable administrative action is being taken in accordance with the example at Appendix L, which includes sample letters and enclosures. The SOR shall be as comprehensive and detailed as the protection of sources afforded confidentiality under provisions of the Privacy Act of 1974 (reference (m)) and national security permit. The statement will contain, 1) a summary of the security concerns and supporting adverse information, 2) instructions for responding to the SOR and 3) copies of the relevant security guidelines from Appendix I. In addition, the CAF will provide within 30 calendar days, upon request of the individual, copies of releasable records of the personnel security investigation (the CAF must retain copies of the file for at least 90 days to ensure the ready availability of the material for the subject). If the CAF is unable to provide requested documents for reasons beyond their control, then the name and address of the agency (agencies) to which the individual may write to obtain a copy of the records will be provided.

(1) The head of the local organization of the individual receiving an SOR shall designate a point of contact (POC) to serve as a liaison between the CAF and the individual. The duties of the POC will include, but not necessarily be limited to, delivering the SOR, having the individual acknowledge receipt of the SOR, determining whether the individual intends to respond within the time specified; ensuring that the individual understands the consequences of the proposed action as well as the consequences for failing to respond in a timely fashion; explaining how to obtain time extensions, procure copies of investigative records, and the procedures for responding to the SOR; and ensuring that the individual understands that he or she can obtain legal counselor *[sic]* other assistance at his or her own expense.

b. Afforded an opportunity to reply in writing to the CAF within 30 calendar days from the date of receipt of the SOR. Failure to submit a timely response will result in forfeiture of all future appeal rights with regard to the unfavorable administrative action. Exceptions to this policy may only be granted by the CAP [Component CAF] in extraordinary circumstances where the individual's failure to respond to the SOR was due to factors beyond his or her control. The CAP must be notified of the individual's intent to respond, via the POC, within 10 calendar days of receipt of the SOR. An extension of up to 30 calendar days may be granted by the employing organization following submission of a written request from the individual. Additional extensions may only be granted by the CAP. Responses to the CAP must be forwarded through the head of the employing organization.

33

c. Provided a written response by the CAP to any submission under subparagraph b. stating the final reason(s) for the unfavorable administrative action, which shall be as specific as privacy and national security considerations permit and in accordance with the example of a letter of denial (LOD) and its enclosures at Appendix L. Such response shall be as prompt as individual circumstances permit, not to exceed 60 calendar days from the date of receipt of the response submitted under subparagraph b., above, provided no additional investigative action is necessary. If a final response cannot be completed within the time frame allowed, the individual must be notified in writing of this fact, the reasons therefore, and the date a final response is expected, which shall not normally exceed a total of 90 days from the date of receipt of the response under subparagraph b.

d. Afforded an opportunity to appeal an LOD, issued pursuant to paragraph c. above, to the component Personnel Security Appeals Board (PSAB). The PSAB shall consist of a minimum of three members and function in accordance with Appendix M. If a decision is made to appeal the LOD, the individual may do so by one of the following methods:

(1) Appeal Without a Personal Appearance: Advise the PSAB within 10 calendar days of receipt of the LOD, of the intent to appeal. Within 40 calendar days of receipt of the LOD, write to the appropriate PSAB stating reasons why the LOD should be overturned and providing any additional relevant information that may have a bearing on the final decision by the PSAB;

(2) Appeal With a Personal Appearance: Advise the Defense Office of Hearings and Appeals (DOHA within 10 calendar days of receipt of the LOD that a personal appearance before a DOHA Administrative Judge (AJ) is desired in order to provide additional, relevant information which may have a bearing on the final decision by the PSAB. DOHA will promptly schedule a personal appearance and will provide a recommendation to the PSAB generally within 60 days of receipt of the notice requesting the personal appearance. Procedures governing the conduct of the personal appearance before a DOHA AJ are contained at Appendix N.

e. Provided a final written decision by the PSAB, including a rationale, to any submission under subparagraph d., above, stating the final disposition of the appeal. This will normally be accomplished within 60 calendar days of receipt of the written appeal from the individual if no personal appearance was requested, or within 30 calendar days from receipt of the AJ's recommendation if a personal appearance was requested.

Appendix N, Conduct of a Personal Appearance Before an Administrative Judge (AJ)

1. A person appealing a Letter of Denial (LOD) may request a personal appearance by notifying the Defense Office of Hearings and Appeals (DOHA) in writing at the following address: Director, Defense Office of Hearings and Appeals, Post Office Box 3656, Arlington, Virginia 22203 (FAX No. 703-696-6865). The request must be sent to DOHA within 10 calendar days

of receipt of the LOD. An extension of time may be granted by the Director, DOHA or designee for good cause demonstrated by the appellant.

2. Upon receipt of a request for a personal appearance, DOHA shall promptly request the appellant's case file from the appropriate CAF, assign the case to an AJ, and provide a copy of the request to the appropriate PSAB. The CAF shall provide the case file to DOHA normally within 10 calendar days.

3. The AJ will schedule a personal appearance generally within 30 calendar days from receipt of the request and arrange for a verbatim transcript of the proceedings. For appellants at duty stations within the lower 48 states, the personal appearance will be conducted at the appellant's duty station or a nearby suitable location. For individuals assigned to duty stations outside the lower 48 states, the personal appearance will be conducted at the appellant's duty station or a nearby suitable location, or at DOHA facilities located in the Washington, D.C. metropolitan area or the Los Angeles, California metropolitan area as determined by the Director, DOHA, or designee.

4. Travel costs for the appellant will be the responsibility of the employing organization.

5. The AJ will conduct the personal appearance proceedings in a fair and orderly manner:

    a. The appellant may be represented by counsel or personal representative at his own expense;

    b. The appellant may make an oral presentation and respond to questions posed by his counsel or personal representative, and shall respond to questions asked by the AJ;

    c. The appellant may submit documents relative to whether the LOD should be overturned;

    d. The appellant will not have the opportunity to present or cross-examine witnesses;

    e. Upon completion of the personal appearance, the AJ will generally forward, within 30 calendar days, a written recommendation to the appropriate PSAB on whether to sustain or overturn the LOD, along with the case file and any documents submitted by the appellant. A copy of the AJ recommendation will be provided to the CAF.

6. The PSAB will render a final written determination stating its rationale and notify the individual in writing (through the individual's employing organization) generally within 30 calendar days of receipt of the recommendation from DOHA. This will be final and will conclude the appeal process.

Appendix D3. Executive Order No. 10865, Sections 3 and 4

Section 3. Except as provided in section 9 of this order, an authorization for access to a specific classification category may not be finally denied or revoked by the head of the department or his designee, including, but not limited to, those officials named in section 8 of this order, unless the applicant has been given the following:

(1) A written statement of the reasons why his access authorization may be denied or revoked, which shall be as comprehensive and detailed as the national security permits.

(2) A reasonable opportunity to reply in writing under oath or affirmation to the statement of reasons.

(3) After he has filed under oath or affirmation a written reply to the statement of reasons, the form and sufficiency of which may be prescribed by regulations issued by the head of the department concerned, an opportunity to appear personally before the head of the department concerned or his designee, including, but not limited to, those officials named in section 8 of this order, for the purpose of supporting his eligibility for access authorization and to present evidence on his behalf.

(4) A reasonable time to prepare for that appearance.

(5) An opportunity to be represented by counsel.

(6) An opportunity to cross-examine persons either orally or through written interrogatories in accordance with section 4 on matters not relating to the characterization in the statement of reasons of any organization or individual other than the applicant.

(7) A written notice of the final decision in his case which, if adverse, shall specify whether the head of the department or his designee, including, but not limited to, those officials named in section 8 of this order, found for or against him with respect to each allegation in the statement of reasons.

Section 4. (a) An applicant shall be afforded an opportunity to cross-examine persons who have made oral or written statements adverse to the applicant relating to a controverted issue except that any such statement may be received and considered without affording such opportunity in the circumstances described in either of the following paragraphs:

(1) The head of the department supplying the statement certifies that the person who furnished the information is a confidential informant who has been engaged in obtaining intelligence information for the Government and that disclosure of his identity would be substantially harmful to the national interest.

(2) The head of the department concerned or his special designee for that particular purpose has preliminarily determined, after considering information furnished by the investigative agency involved as to the reliability of the person and the accuracy of the statement concerned, that the statement concerned appears to be reliable and material, and the head of the department or such special designee has determined that failure to receive and consider such statement would, in view of the level of access sought, be substantially harmful to the national security and that the person who furnished the information cannot appear to testify (A) due to death, severe illness, or similar cause, in which case the identity of the person and the information to be considered shall be made available to the applicant, or (B) due to some other cause determined by the head of the department to be good and sufficient.

(b) Whenever procedures under paragraph (1) or (2) of subsection (a) of this section are used (1) the applicant shall be given a summary of the information which shall be as comprehensive and detailed as the national security permits, (2) appropriate consideration shall be accorded to the fact that the applicant did not have an opportunity to cross-examine such person or persons, and (3) a final determination adverse to the applicant shall be made only by the head of the department based upon his personal review of the case.

Appendix D4. DoDD 5220.6, Sections 4.3. and 4.4. and Enclosure E3, Sections E3.1.1. through E3.1.36.6.

4. POLICY

4.3. Except as otherwise provided for by E.O. [Executive Order] 10865 (enclosure 1) or this Directive, a final unfavorable clearance decision shall not be made without first providing the applicant with:

4.3.1. Notice of specific reasons for the proposed action.

4.3.2. An opportunity to respond to the reasons.

4.3.3. Notice of the right to a hearing and the opportunity to cross-examine persons providing information adverse to the applicant.

4.3.4. Opportunity to present evidence on his or her own behalf, or to be represented by counsel or personal representative.

4.3.5. Written notice of final clearance decisions.

4.3.6. Notice of appeal procedures.

4.4. Actions pursuant to this Directive shall cease upon termination of the applicant's need for access to classified information except in those cases in which:

4.4.1. A hearing has commenced;

4.4.2. A clearance decision has been issued; or

4.4.3. The applicant's security clearance was suspended and the applicant provided a written request that the case continue.

E3. ENCLOSURE 3, ADDITIONAL PROCEDURAL GUIDANCE

E3.1.1. When the DISCO cannot affirmatively find that it is clearly consistent with the national interest to grant or continue a security clearance for an applicant, the case shall be promptly referred to the DOHA.

E3.1.2. Upon referral, the DOHA shall make a prompt determination whether to grant or continue a security clearance, issue a statement of reasons (SOR) as to why it is not clearly consistent with the national interest to do so, or take interim actions, including but not limited to:

E3.1.2.1. Direct further investigation.

E3.1.2.2. Propound written interrogatories to the applicant or other persons with relevant information.

E3.1.2.3. Requiring the applicant to undergo a medical evaluation by a DoD Psychiatric Consultant.

E3.1.2.4. Interviewing the applicant.

E3.1.3. An unfavorable clearance decision shall not be made unless the applicant has been provided with a written SOR that shall be as detailed and comprehensive as the national security permits. A letter of instruction with the SOR shall explain that the applicant or Department Counsel may request a hearing. It shall also explain the adverse consequences for failure to respond to the SOR within the prescribed time frame.

E3.1.4. The applicant must submit a detailed written answer to the SOR under oath or affirmation that shall admit or deny each listed allegation. A general denial or other similar answer is insufficient. To be entitled to a hearing, the applicant must specifically request a hearing in his or her answer. The answer must be received by the DOHA within 20 days from receipt of the SOR. Requests for an extension of time to file an answer may be submitted to the Director, DOHA, or designee, who in turn may grant the extension only upon a showing of good cause.

E3.1.5. If the applicant does not file a timely and responsive answer to the SOR, the Director, DOHA, or designee, may discontinue processing the case, deny issuance of the requested security clearance, and direct the DISCO to revoke any security clearance held by the applicant.

E3.1.6. Should review of the applicant's answer to the SOR indicate that allegations are unfounded, or evidence is insufficient for further processing, Department Counsel shall take such action as appropriate under the circumstances, including but not limited to withdrawal of the SOR and transmittal to the Director for notification of the DISCO for appropriate action.

E3.1.7. If the applicant has not requested a hearing with his or her answer to the SOR and Department Counsel has not requested a hearing within 20 days of receipt of the applicant's answer, the case shall be assigned to the Administrative Judge for a clearance decision based on the written record. Department Counsel shall provide the applicant with a copy of all relevant and material information that could be adduced at a hearing. The applicant shall have 30 days from receipt of the information in which to submit a documentary response setting forth objections, rebuttal, extenuation, mitigation, or explanation, as appropriate.

E3.1.8. If a hearing is requested by the applicant or Department Counsel, the case shall be assigned to the Administrative Judge for a clearance decision based on the hearing record. Following issuance of a notice of hearing by the Administrative Judge, or designee, the applicant shall appear in person with or without counsel or a personal representative at a time and place designated by the notice of hearing. The applicant shall have a reasonable amount of time to prepare his or her case. The applicant shall be notified at least 15 days in advance of the time and place of the hearing, which generally shall be held at a location in the United States within a metropolitan area near the applicant's place of employment or residence. A continuance may be granted by the Administrative Judge only for good cause. Hearings may be held outside of the United States in NATO [North Atlantic Treaty Organization] cases, or in other cases upon a finding of good cause by the Director, DOHA, or designee.

E3.1.9. The Administrative Judge may require a pre-hearing conference.

E3.1.10. The Administrative Judge may rule on questions on procedure, discovery, and evidence and shall conduct all proceedings in a fair, timely, and orderly manner.

E3.1.11. Discovery by the applicant is limited to non-privileged documents and materials subject to control by the DOHA. Discovery by Department Counsel after issuance of an SOR may be granted by the Administrative Judge only upon a showing of good cause.

E3.1.12. A hearing shall be open except when the applicant requests that it be closed, or when the Administrative Judge determines that there is a need to protect classified information or there is only good cause for keeping the proceeding closed. No inference shall be drawn as to the merits of a case on the basis of a request that the hearing be closed.

E3.1.13. As far in advance as practical, Department Counsel and the applicant shall serve one another with a copy of any pleading, proposed documentary evidence, or other written communication to be submitted to the Administrative Judge.

E3.1.14. Department Counsel is responsible for presenting witnesses and other evidence to establish facts alleged in the SOR that have been controverted.

E3.1.15. The applicant is responsible for presenting witnesses and other evidence to rebut, explain, extenuate, or mitigate facts admitted by the applicant or proven by Department Counsel, and has the ultimate burden of persuasion as to obtaining a favorable clearance decision.

E3.1.16. Witnesses shall be subject to cross-examination.

E3.1.17. The SOR may be amended at the hearing by the Administrative Judge on his or her own motion, or upon motion by Department Counsel or the applicant, so as to render it in conformity with the evidence admitted or for other good cause. When such amendments are made, the Administrative Judge may grant either party's request for such additional time as the Administrative Judge may deem appropriate for further preparation or other good cause.

E3.1.18. The Administrative Judge hearing the case shall notify the applicant and all witnesses testifying that 18 U.S.C. 1001 (reference (c)) is applicable.

E3.1.19. The Federal Rules of Evidence (28 U.S.C. 101 et seq. (reference (d)) shall serve as a guide. Relevant and material evidence may be received subject to rebuttal, and technical rules of evidence may be relaxed, except as otherwise provided herein, to permit the development of a full and complete record.

E3.1.20. Official records or evidence compiled or created in the regular course of business, other than DoD personnel background reports of investigation (ROI), may be received and considered by the Administrative Judge without authenticating witnesses, provided that such information has been furnished by an investigative agency pursuant to its responsibilities in connection with assisting the Secretary of Defense, or the Department or Agency head concerned, to safeguard classified information within industry under E.O. 10865 (enclosure 1.). An ROI may be received with an authenticating witness provided it is otherwise admissible under the Federal Rules of Evidence (28 U.S.C. 101 et seq. (reference (d)).

E3.1.21. Records that cannot be inspected by the applicant because they are classified may be received and considered by the Administrative Judge, provided the GC [General Counsel], DoD, has:

E3.1.21.1. Made a preliminary determination that such evidence appears to be relevant and material.

E3.1.21.2. Determined that failure to receive and consider such evidence would be substantially harmful to the national security.

E3.1.22. A written or oral statement adverse to the applicant on a controverted issue may be received and considered by the Administrative Judge without affording an opportunity to cross-examine the person making the statement orally, or in writing when justified by the circumstances, only in either of the following circumstances:

E3.1.22.1 If the head of the Department or Agency supplying the statement certifies that the person who furnished the information is a confidential informant who has been engaged in obtaining intelligence information for the Government and that disclosure of his or her identity would be substantially harmful to the national interest; or

E3.1.22.2. If the GC, DoD, has determined the statement concerned appears to be relevant, material, and reliable; failure to receive and consider the statement would be substantially harmful to the national security; and the person who furnished the information cannot appear to testify due to the following:

E3.1.22.2.1. Death, severe illness, or similar cause, in which case the identity of the person and the information to be considered shall be made available to the applicant; or

E3.1.22.2.2 Some other cause determined by the Secretary of Defense, or when appropriate by the Department or Agency head, to be good and sufficient.

E3.1.23. Whenever evidence is received under items E3.1.21. or E3.1.22., above, the applicant shall be furnished with as comprehensive and detailed a summary of

41

the information as the national security permits. The Administrative Judge and Appeal Board may make a clearance decision either favorable or unfavorable to the applicant based on such evidence after giving appropriate consideration to the fact that the applicant did not have an opportunity to confront such evidence, but any final determination adverse to the applicant shall be made only by the Secretary of Defense, or the Department or Agency head, based on a personal review of the case record.

E3.1.24. A verbatim transcript shall be made of the hearing. The applicant shall be furnished one copy of the transcript, less the exhibits, without cost.

E3.1.25. The Administrative Judge shall make a written clearance decision in a timely manner setting forth pertinent findings of fact, policies, and conclusions as to the allegations in the SOR, and whether it is clearly consistent with the national interest to grant or continue a security clearance for the applicant. The applicant and Department Counsel shall each be provided a copy of the clearance decision. In cases in which evidence is received under items E3.1.21. and E3.1.22., above the Administrative Judge's written clearance decision may require deletions in the interest of national security.

E3.1.26. If the Administrative Judge decides that it is clearly consistent with the national interest for the applicant to be granted or to retain a security clearance, the DISCO shall be so notified by the Director, DOHA, or designee, when the clearance decision becomes final in accordance with item E3.1.36., below.

E3.1.27. If the Administrative Judge decides that it is not clearly consistent with the national interest for the applicant to be granted or to retain a security clearance, the Director, DOHA, or designee, shall expeditiously notify the DISCO, which shall in turn notify the applicant's employer of the denial or revocation of the applicant's security clearance. The letter forwarding the Administrative Judge's clearance decision to the applicant shall advise the applicant that these actions are being taken, and that the applicant may appeal the Administrative Judge's clearance decision.

E3.1.28. The applicant or Department Counsel may appeal the Administrative Judge's clearance decision by filing a written notice of appeal with the Appeal Board within 15 days after the date of the Administrative Judge's clearance decision. A notice of appeal received after 15 days from the date of the clearance decision shall not be accepted by the Appeal Board, or designated Board Member, except for good cause. A notice of cross-appeal may be filed with the Appeal Board within 10 days of receipt of the notice of appeal. An untimely cross-appeal shall not be accepted by the Appeal Board, or designated Board Member, except for good cause.

E3.1.29. Upon receipt of a notice of appeal, the Appeal Board shall be provided the case record. No new evidence shall be received or considered by the Appeal Board.

E3.1.30. After filing a timely notice of appeal, a written appeal brief must be received by the Appeal Board within 45 days from the date of the Administrative Judge's clearance decision. The appeal brief must state the specific issue or issues being raised, and cite specific portions of the case record supporting any alleged error. A written reply brief, if any, must be filed within 20 days from receipt of the appeal brief. A copy of any brief filed must be served upon the applicant or Department Counsel, as appropriate.

E3.1.31. Requests for extension of time for submission of briefs may be submitted to the Appeal Board or designated Board Member. A copy of any request for extension of time must be served on the opposing party at the time of submission. The Appeal Board, or designated Board Member, shall be responsible for controlling the Appeal Board's docket, and may enter an order dismissing an appeal in an appropriate case or vacate such an order upon a showing of good cause

E3.1.32. The Appeal Board shall address the material issues raised by the parties to determine whether harmful error occurred. Its scope of review shall be to determine whether or not:

E3.1.32.1. The Administrative Judge's findings of fact are supported by such relevant evidence as a reasonable mind might accept as adequate to support a conclusion in light of all the contrary evidence in the same record. In making this review, the Appeal Board shall give deference to the credibility determinations of the Administrative Judge;

E3.1.32.2. The Administrative Judge adhered to the procedures required by E.O. 10865 (enclosure 1.) and this Directive; or

E3.1.32.3. The Administrative Judge's rulings or conclusions are arbitrary, capricious, or contrary to law.

E3.1.33. The Appeal Board shall issue a written clearance decision addressing the material issues raised on appeal. The Appeal Board shall have authority to:

E3.1.33.1 Affirm the decision of the Administrative Judge;

E3.1.33.2. Remand the case to an Administrative Judge to correct identified error. If the case is remanded, the Appeal Board shall specify the action to be taken on remand; or

E3.1.33.3. Reverse the decision of the Administrative Judge if correction of identified error mandates such action.

E3.1.34. A copy of the Appeal Board's written clearance decision shall be provided to the parties. In cases in which evidence was received under items E3.1.21. and E3.1.22., above, the Appeal Board's clearance decision may require deletions in the interest of national security.

E3.1.35. Upon remand, the case file shall be assigned to a Administrative Judge for correction of error(s) in accordance with the Appeal Board's clearance decision. The assigned Administrative Judge shall make a new clearance decision in the case after correcting the error(s) identified by the Appeal Board. The

Administrative Judge's clearance decision after remand shall be provided to the parties. The clearance decision after remand may be appealed pursuant to items E3.1.28. to E3.1.35., above.

E3.1.36. A clearance decision shall be considered final when:

E3.1.36.1. A security clearance is granted or continued pursuant to item E3.1.2., above;

E3.1.36.2 No timely notice of appeal is filed;

E3.1.36.3. No timely appeal brief is filed after a notice of appeal has been filed;

E3.1.36.4. The appeal has been withdrawn:

E3.1.36.5. When the Appeal Board affirms or reverses an Administrative Judge's clearance decision; or

E3.1.36.6. When a decision has been made by the Secretary of Defense, or the Department or Agency head, under item E3.1.23., above. The Director, DOHA, or designee, shall notify the DISCO of all final clearance decisions.

Appendix E. Personnel Security Appeal Boards

DoD 5200.2-R allows the individual CAFs discretion to choose their members, the manner of their selection, and their length of service. The Army, Navy, Air Force, and WHS PSABs are all operated differently.

Army

The president and permanent member of the Army PSAB does not have a personnel security background. This is not in full compliance with DoD 5200.2-R, which requires that the president be both a permanent member and have a security background. However, the nonvoting executive secretary does have a background in personnel security. The 2 additional members are selected on rotational basis from among 10 individuals employed by the offices of the Deputy Chief of Staff for Operations and Plans, the Deputy Chief of Staff for Logistics, the Assistant Chief of Staff for Installation Management, the Chief of the Army Reserve, and the National Guard Bureau. This rotation allows individuals to attend about 3-4 meetings per year. The Army also allows members access to legal counsel when necessary rather than appointing a member to the board. The counsel for the Army does not attend all meetings but is contacted by the board most frequently by telephone or e-mail.

Navy

The permanent member of the Navy PSAB is the president and has a security background. The two additional members include a member of the military that is at least at the O-6 level with an intelligence or an operations background, and the other member is a civilian that is at least a GS/GM-14 with a personnel background. Access to legal counsel, psychologists, and counterintelligence specialists are provided by the Naval Criminal Investigative Service.

Air Force

All members of the Air Force PSAB are permanent members. The Air Force PSAB president has a legal background rather than a security background. This does not fully comply with DoD 5200.2-R; however, the other two members of the board have a security and an intelligence background.

Washington Headquarters Services

The permanent member of the WHS PSAB is the president and has a security background. The two additional members are chosen from employees of the Office of the Secretary of Defense and employees from the same agency from which the applicant is seeking to appeal. The agency representative is appointed to ensure that the unique program and management interests of the agency are represented during board deliberations. The WHS chose to allow members to have access to legal counsel rather than appoint a lawyer as a member. The legal counsel available to the WHS PSAB is present at the meetings for any legal inquiries members may have.

Appendix F. Report Distribution

Office of the Secretary of Defense

Under Secretary of Defense for Acquisition, Technology, and Logistics
    Director, Special Programs
    Chairman, Business Initiative Council
Under Secretary of Defense (Comptroller)/Chief Financial Officer
    Deputy Chief Financial Officer
    Deputy Comptroller (Program/Budget)
Under Secretary of Defense for Intelligence
    Deputy Under Secretary of Defense (Security and Information Operations)
        Director, Security
            Deputy Director, Personnel Security
General Counsel of the Department of Defense
    Deputy General Counsel, Legal Counsel
    Director, Defense Office of Hearing and Appeals
Director, Washington Headquarters Services
    Director, Directorate for Personnel and Security
        Chief, Consolidated Adjudication Facility
        President, Clearance Appeal Board, Security Division

Joint Staff

Director, Joint Staff
    Director of Management
        Chief, Personnel Security Branch, Joint Staff Security Office

Department of the Army

Chief, Army Technology Management Office, Director of the Army Staff
Auditor General, Department of the Army
Commander, Army Central Personnel Security Clearance Facility, Intelligence and
    Security Command
President, Personnel Security Appeal Board, Assistant Secretary of the Army (Manpower
    and Reserve Affairs)

Department of the Navy

Naval Inspector General
Director, Special Programs Division, Chief of Naval Operations
President, Personnel Security Appeal Board, Chief of Naval Operations
Superintendent, Naval Postgraduate School
Auditor General, Department of the Navy
Director, Naval Criminal Investigative Service
    Director, Central Adjudication Facility

Department of the Air Force

Administrative Assistant to the Secretary of the Air Force
  Director, Security and Special Programs Oversight
  Director, Air Force Central Adjudication Facility
Auditor General, Department of the Air Force
President, Personnel Security Appeal Board, General Law Division, Judge Advocate
  General

Other Defense Organizations

Director, Defense Intelligence Agency
  Chief, Central Adjudication Facility, Counter Intelligence and Security Activities,
    Directorate for Administration
  Inspector General, Defense Intelligence Agency
Director, Defense Security Service
  Inspector General, Defense Security Service
  Director, Defense Industrial Security Clearance Office
Director, National Security Agency
  Chief, Central Adjudication Facility, Personnel Security Analysis, Security Services
    Directorate
  Inspector General, National Security Agency
Inspector General, National Imagery and Mapping Agency

Non-Defense Federal Organization

Office of Management and Budget

Congressional Committees and Subcommittees, Chairman and Ranking Minority Member

Senate Committee on Appropriations
Senate Subcommittee on Defense, Committee on Appropriations
Senate Committee on Armed Services
Senate Committee on Governmental Affairs
Senate Select Committee on Intelligence
House Committee on Appropriations
House Subcommittee on Defense, Committee on Appropriations
House Committee on Armed Services
House Committee on Government Reform
House Subcommittee on Government Efficiency and Financial Management, Committee
  on Government Reform
House Subcommittee on National Security, Emerging Threats, and International
  Relations, Committee on Government Reform
House Subcommittee on Technology, Information Policy, Intergovernmental Relations,
  and the Census, Committee on Government Reform
House Permanent Select Committee on Intelligence

Office of the Under Secretary of Defense for Intelligence Comments

OFFICE OF THE UNDER SECRETARY OF DEFENSE
5000 DEFENSE PENTAGON
WASHINGTON, DC 20301-5000

August 21, 2003

INTELLIGENCE

MEMORANDUM FOR DEPUTY ASSISTANT INSPECTOR GENERAL FOR AUDITING

SUBJECT: DoD Security Clearance Adjudication and Appeal Process, Project No. D1999AD-0079.05

This memorandum is in response to a request for review and comment to the draft version of this report. Unfortunately, the report is confusing. Its lack of clarity leads to a misunderstanding of the adjudicative process. The recommendations are generic and applicable to almost every government program. The report offers neither a persuasive basis to establish a single process nor a rationale for a single directive. The report does not validate the recommendations.

The Department is embarked on a major effort to improve its personnel security program. The personnel security investigative function will be transferred to the Office of Personnel Management (OPM) in FY04. The Department will transition from the EPSQ to the Electronic Questionnaires for Investigations Processing (e-QIP) when programming between DoD and OPM is completed in FY04. A review of the adjudication process is underway and targeted for completion this fall. The review will not only consider process issues but the realignment of adjudicative responsibilities and opportunities to automate the process. The Department has proposed changes to the adjudication guidelines to the inter-agency working group charted to look at personnel security policy issues. Additionally, there is a proposed congressionally directed action tasking the Director of the Central Intelligence Agency and the Secretary of Defense to submit a joint report to Congress on the utility and effectiveness of the current security background investigations and security clearance procedures of the Federal Government in meeting the purposes of such investigations and procedures. These initiatives provide a more comprehensive approach to improving the DoD personnel security program.

Carol A. Haave
Deputy Assistant Secretary of Defense
(Security and Information Operations)

Office of the General Counsel of the Department of Defense Comments

DEPARTMENT OF DEFENSE
OFFICE OF GENERAL COUNSEL
1600 DEFENSE PENTAGON
WASHINGTON, DC 20301-1600

3 0 JUL 2003

MEMORANDUM FOR THE INSPECTOR GENERAL

SUBJECT: DoD Security Clearance Adjudication and Appeal Process,
Project No. D1999AD-0079.05

This memorandum responds to the final version of this report presented to us for comment. Unfortunately, for the reasons set out below, the analysis contained in the report is fundamentally flawed and infused with major factual errors and misconceptions. Two of the more serious ones are discussed below. The recommendations, though based on this flawed analysis, are acceptable in part.

First, the report is internally inconsistent in adopting an idiosyncratic analysis of the adjudication and appeal process, and it makes a fundamental error in the description of this process and the comparison of the procedures available to contractor employees on the one hand and military personnel and government employees on the other. The report erroneously equates two very different actions: referring a contractor employee's case for further processing and issuing a Letter of Denial to government employees and military personnel. This is incorrect as a matter of fact and as a matter of law, and this error alone essentially destroys the value of the analysis contained in the report. Moreover, this error underlines continuing and persistent confusion in discussion of the adjudication and appeal process: for example, it leads to a conclusion that there is an extra step in one of these processes and to a discussion of the issue of the availability of relevant documents to the individual that is virtually incomprehensible.

The report also presents a misleading description of the organization and legal structure of the adjudication facilities within the Department. The components with delegated authority to establish adjudication facilities have not placed them in the same places within their various organization structures, but in each case the adjudication facility is separate from the chain of command over the vast majority of the individuals whose clearances are adjudicated. Each component has a Personnel Security Appeals Board that operates separately from the adjudication facility. The Defense Office of Hearings and Appeals (DOHA), which conducts the adjudication and appeal process for contractor employees, also divides the adjudication and appeal authority, vesting adjudication in personnel security specialists and Administrative Judges and appellate authority in its Appeals Board. Both the component adjudication facilities and DOHA operate under rules and in an environment that protects their impartiality and independence from improper efforts to influence decisions in individual cases. Both organizational approaches are legally sound, allow appropriate management and supervision within the Department, and have been successfully defended in litigation.

50

I regret the necessity to provide comments of this nature, but allowing these errors, and others in the report, to stand without response could open the door for potentially serious adverse consequences for the Department. Your staff has consulted with various officials in the Department repeatedly in researching and drafting this report, and their efforts and goals are commendable, though unfortunately flawed. I hope that in future projects we will be able to work together more successfully.

The following are my comments on the recommendations:

Recommendation 1: Reengineer the adjudication and appeal process by establishing a single, common security clearance process for military, civilian, and contractor employees.

Response: Concur that a review of the adjudication and appeal process is appropriate but non-concur with the recommendation that the result must be a single process applicable to both groups.

The report notes that the contractor process differs from the process for government employees and military personnel, but it provides no rationale for the need to unify them. Contractor employees hold a different legal status from both government employees and military personnel, and the procedures available to them in a wide range of dealings with the government differ significantly from those available to individuals who have a direct employment relationship with the government. As the report's analysis is fundamentally flawed, there is no persuasive basis for the recommendation to establish a single process.

Recommendation 2: Develop a single directive or regulation for the DoD security clearance program.

Response: Concur that a review of the regulations governing the security clearance program is appropriate but non-concur with the recommendation that the result must be a single directive or regulation applicable to both groups. While simplifying and combining multiple documents providing guidance has a certain facial appeal, as with the first recommendation, the report offers no rationale for a single directive. The current regulatory structure, which is not discussed in detail in the report, appears to work well; it does not seem to cause confusion among those who use these regulations.

Paul W. Cobb, Jr.

Paul W. Cobb, Jr.
Deputy General Counsel
(Legal Counsel)

Team Members

Personnel of the Office of the Inspector General of the Department of Defense who contributed to the report are listed below.

Thomas F. Gimble
Robert K. West
Lois A. Therrien
Sheri D. Dillard
Mary A. Hoover
Eric G. Fisher
Jacqueline N. Pugh